LIVING IN THE SPIRIT

THE CHURCH'S TEACHING SERIES

Prepared at the request of the Executive Council of the General Convention of the Episcopal Church

1 CHRISTIAN BELIEVING
Urban T. Holmes III
John H. Westerhoff III

2 THE BIBLE FOR TODAY'S CHURCH
Robert A. Bennett
O. C. Edwards

3 THE CHURCH IN HISTORY
John E. Booty

4 UNDERSTANDING THE FAITH OF THE CHURCH
Richard A. Norris

5 LITURGY FOR LIVING
Charles P. Price
Louis Weil

6 THE CHRISTIAN MORAL VISION
Earl H. Brill

7 LIVING IN THE SPIRIT
Rachel Hosmer
Alan Jones

LIVING IN
THE SPIRIT

Written by
Rachel Hosmer and Alan Jones
with the assistance of a group of
editorial advisors under the direction of the
Church's Teaching Series Committee

1817

Harper & Row, Publishers, San Francisco

New York, Grand Rapids, Philadelphia, St. Louis
London, Singapore, Sydney, Tokyo, Toronto

Library of Congress Catalog Card Number: 79-26121
ISBN: 0-86683-907-0

89 90 91 92 93 94 MCN 10 9 8 7 6 5 4

Foreword

The series of books published for the most part in the 1950s and known as the Church's Teaching Series has had a profound effect on the life and work of the Episcopal Church during the past twenty years. It is a monumental credit to that original series and to the authors and editors of those volumes that the Church has seen fit to produce a new set of books to be known by the same name. Though the volumes will be different in style and content, the concern for quality education that prompts the issuing of the new series is the same, for the need of Church members for knowledge in areas of scripture, theology, liturgy, history, and ethics is a need that continues from age to age.

I recommend this new Church's Teaching Series to all who seek to know the Lord Jesus and to know the great tradition that he has commended to us.

John M. Allin
PRESIDING BISHOP

Introduction

This is one of a series of volumes in the new Church's Teaching Series. The project has been both challenging and exciting. Not only is there a wide variety of opinions regarding the substance of the teaching of the Church, there are also varying and conflicting views with regard to the methods of communicating this teaching to others. That is why we have tried to pay close attention to the various movements within the Church, and to address them. The development of this new series, therefore, has involved hundreds of men and women throughout the Episcopal Church and is offered as one resource among many for the purposes of Christian education.

While it is neither possible nor perhaps even desirable today to produce a definitive series of books setting forth the specific teachings of a particular denomination, we have tried to emphasize the element of continuity between this new series and the old. Continuity, however, implies movement, and we believe that the new series breaks fresh ground in a creative and positive way.

The new series makes modest claims. It speaks not so much *for* the Episcopal Church as *to* it, and not to this Church only but to Christians of other traditions, and to those who wait expectantly at the edge of the Church.

Two words have been in constant use to describe this project from its inception: affirmation and exploration. The writers have affirmed the great insights of the Christian tradition and have also explored new possibilities for the future in the confidence that the future is God's.

Alan Jones
CHAIRMAN OF THE
CHURCH'S TEACHING SERIES
COMMITTEE

The authors of *Living in the Spirit* wish to express their deep gratitude to John H. Westerhoff III for his contribution to the final form of the manuscript.

LIVING IN THE SPIRIT

Contents

Part One

THE REVELATION
OF HUMAN MEANING

· 1 ·

The Beginning of Life

Nine months of waiting, and now the time has come. The baby is about to be born. The mother, her abdomen swollen with new life, looks up and smiles at her husband by her side. She is glad to have him there. His presence somehow helps her to surrender to that movement of life struggling within her.

She wonders what the outcome will be of their coming together in love. Will it be a boy or a girl? It doesn't matter. Will it be strong and healthy? "Oh, I pray so, with all my heart!" Another contraction. The mother takes a deep breath and concentrates. The baby is very active now. New life struggles within the woman, beyond her control. The fetal monitor bleeps frantically, recording every movement within her. The baby's heartbeat is strong. A wire is attached to the baby's head that is linked to the monitor. Any distress inside the womb will be spotted at once. "All this machinery!" thinks the father.

"I have to push!" cries the mother, and with a burst of activity she is edged onto a stretcher-bed and wheeled into the delivery room. The father hurriedly exchanges his yellow paper overall for a green cloth one. It is all so sudden. At one moment the baby was not there. Now he is. Yes—it's a boy and a fine, healthy one. The monitor wire is still attached to his head. There was no time to remove it. It waves to and fro. The new baby looks like a space-child floating free of his mother-ship. As the doctor cuts the cord, the child is really free yet helpless. What will become of him? What can it all be for? What can it possibly mean? Can *he* mean anything? Does it matter?

There he floats, the newborn baby. He looks so vulnerable. His face and body are mottled and shrunken as if he were anticipating old age. Indeed he is already on the road to death and dissolution. In fact, he looks like a frail little old man even now. His hands are shriveled and his face and limbs twisted: signs of death in this new life. Can there be anything more than that? Can there be energies other than life-moving-towards-death at work in him? Is death the end? Is there a God? If there is a God, does he care?

What does it mean to be and become a human being? This is the basic concern of this book. The answers we give are rooted in the Christian understanding of what a human being essentially is: a child of God. The newborn baby is indeed marked for death. He is mortal. But the Christian affirms that there is an energy at work in him other than that which pushes him to his death. That other energy is the Holy Spirit—probing, pushing, and challenging each one of us to be more himself.

It is easy to forget that the birth of each new baby is a miracle. It is a unique and unrepeatable gift. Most people take this miracle, this mystery, for granted. Modern medicine, as wonderful as it is, has managed to hide the mystery, to blind us to the miracle of birth with the (often necessary) hygienic procedures of the modern hospital. The beginning of human life is truly awesome. The sense of wonder is so easily lost, yet without it, human life is impoverished. Love grows cold, and we die, little by little, inside. There can be no life-as-movement-beyond-death without this native sense of awe and wonder. It is a requirement for living in the Spirit. It is the heart of Christian prayer. To be open to mystery, beginning with the mystery that *we are*, is what it means to explore the life of prayer. There is more to that newborn baby than his helpless vulnerability, the flopping instability of his head, and the shriveled uselessness of his limbs. He is more than we will ever know and than he will ever know.

This book, then, is about what it means to be and become a human being in the power of the Holy Spirit. Our concern is with spirituality that, for Christians, is life in the Spirit.

Living in the Spirit

What comes into your mind when the word *spirituality* is mentioned? Most people think that it has something to do with the saints, with prayer, with special devotions. It does. But it is much more than that. In the minds of many, whatever spirituality is, it is something remote and certainly not for everyone. Nothing could be further from the truth. If we are to discover what spirituality is about, we will have to give up some of our ideas about it. For example, there are many people who think that spirituality means something different from, or even something in opposition to, the body and the ordinary affairs of this world. Some spiritualities do, indeed, deny the flesh and even *hate* the body. But this is a far cry from true Christian spirituality.

What is Spirituality?

In this volume we are using the word *spirituality* in two ways, one more important, because more universal and more radical than the other. The most important meaning of *spirituality* is that which gives meaning and harmony to the whole of human experience. It is the peculiar way in which we arrange all the bits and pieces of our lives and glue them together. How is that newborn baby going to make sense of all his experiences? The unique way he does it will be his peculiar and special *spirituality*. For us, there is a loving and unifying energy already at work in him: the Spirit of Christ. The link between the baby's world of everyday experience and the creative and transforming Spirit is faith. Not that he understands this yet! Seen as a series of connecting links, spirituality deals with everything in creation. It is the way the growing human being understands how each piece of his or her life and the life of the world is connected with every other.

But spirituality has another meaning. It also focuses upon that part of our experience which we call *spiritual* as distinct from the material (for example, how to cook, what stars are made of, where babies come from), the scientific, and the historical. It is concerned with practical things about what we do to grow up. How do we fit into the scheme of things? What must we do and be to grow as humans in the power of the Holy Spirit?

This book will deal with both meanings—with spirituality as an overview of life and with spirituality as a practical guide to the life of prayer. Indeed, the early Christians were called followers of the Way, and the Christian Way is a journey towards union with God. It is a common journey, a shared adventure, and one that involves a leap of faith into the unknown. The aim of the book is to help deepen, in a practical way, the reader's commitment to Christ, especially through private prayer and in sharing the corporate worship of the church, particularly within the Anglican tradition.

Growing in the Spirit

Having thought about birth, we can now begin to reflect on those events which helped us grow up. Imagine you are a six-year-old again. You are playing with your friends in the woods near your home. At one point you simply decide to wander off by yourself. Suddenly you look up and see you are standing at the foot of a great oak tree. Its branches seem to reach the sky and its roots surely go to the center of the earth. Suddenly an astounding thought comes to you. The tree is a *living thing,* separate from you and infinitely older and wiser. You are both fascinated and a little frightened. Unable to hold onto the experience, you run back to your friends and announce, "Trees are alive! Did you know?" This is probably your first encounter with *is-ness* (there doesn't seem to be any real name for it). It is simply the experience of the living, separate existence of a tree. But an experience like this can have a profound effect on a six-year-old.

And if you think about it, you may remember other

growing experiences. What paths have opened up in front of you? What doors have slammed in your face? What were the events and experiences that led you to want to commit your life to Christ?

There is another important event in a newborn baby's life that is, for us, the sign that there is a mystery, an *otherness* at work in him: his baptism.

The Miracle of Being Born Again

The baby snuggles lazily in his mother's arms. He yawns, screws up his mouth, and moves his head in search of his mother's breast. Three weeks in the world—no worries. His world is almost entirely the breast, the warmth, the pleasant sounds. The church is already partly full when the young family arrives. Grandparents and godparents have saved some seats, and the service is about to begin. In the middle of the aisle, right near the front, is a small table. On it stands a large bowl and a pitcher. By it is a small white towel.

The Christians have gathered on a Sunday morning to break bread together and welcome their newest member. The service begins, and soon the baby is handed over to the priest to be baptized. It is a strange ceremony. The priest, who seems kind enough, takes the baby in his arms. The prayers have been said: "We thank you, Father, for the water of Baptism. In it we are buried with Christ in his death. By it we share in his resurrection." The baby, only a few weeks old, is drowned! The bowl looks too small, but drowning seems to be the priest's intention. The baby is buried in the waters of baptism. His old life is over—the life that pushed and still pushes him towards death. He is dead and buried, and at the moment of his burial there is affirmed the surge of new life. The child is taken from the fumbling but loving hands of his parents and placed in the expansive and loving hands of God. Over him is proclaimed the reality of the power of the Holy Spirit that will pull him through death and beyond. Death is not the end. In adult life, of course, the child will have to make this event his own. Meanwhile, the Christian community has proclaimed that he is not only a child of his earthly parents, but that he is also a child of the One who made the whole universe. There is an *otherness* present within him. We dare to call that *otherness* the Holy Spirit. In fact, in spite of all human silliness and sin (which are real enough), the most real thing about us is the Holy Spirit working at depths within us too deep for words.

Living in the Spirit is concerned with keeping that fire of glory alive and glowing. It is easily suppressed although never entirely quenched. When we grow up, the wonder and the glory are often diminished. What was once a glowing fire becomes a smoking ember. We need to return again and again to our baptism to be reminded of the deep presence of the Holy Spirit.

Christian Baptism, then, is a peculiar event. It is the sacrament of new beginnings. It is a sign of the two energies at work in us: one, the energy of life-towards-death, and the other, the energy of life-towards-greater-life. In our baptism we anticipate our dying, for it is, indeed, a burial service. In it we also anticipate new life by affirming the work of the Holy Spirit. Baptism also calls us into the fellowship of the church, into communion with all those who live in the Spirit. We are truly "members one of another."

Seeing the Kingdom

Now there was a man of the Pharisees, named Nicodemus, a ruler of the Jews. This man came to Jesus by night and said to him, 'Rabbi, we know that you are a teacher come from God; for no one can do these signs that you do, unless God is with him.' Jesus answered him, 'Truly, truly, I say to you, unless one is born anew, he cannot see the kingdom of God.' Nicodemus said to him, 'How can a man be born when he is old? Can he enter a second time into his mother's womb and be born?' Jesus answered, 'Truly, truly, I say to you, unless one is born of water and the Spirit, he cannot enter the kingdom of God. That which is born of the flesh is flesh, and that which is born of the Spirit is spirit. Do not marvel that I said to you, 'You must be born anew' (Jn. 3:1–7).

How do you interpret these words? "Unless one is born anew, he cannot see the kingdom of God." Have you been born anew? What is the mystery of this second birth? Perhaps we are as puzzled by it as Nicodemus was. What is the Kingdom of which Jesus speaks?

Think of those little rebirths in your own experience that caused you to see your life in a totally new light. Such moments are hints of what baptism is all about: like the incident cited of the small child really *seeing* a tree for the first time. The child caught a glimpse of the Kingdom, the place where God reigns.

Christianity is the religion of the reign of God breaking in, creating new possibilities in us and for us. The Christian life is one in which we are continually re-made by the love of God. Part of the Good News is that the newness of God's reign can break in at any time and at any age. "How can a man be born when he is old?" asked Nicodemus. The answer is that he can always be reborn because of that gracious *otherness* that is present in each of us.

· 2 ·

The Mystery of Being Human

Becoming a human being is very hard work—and at the same time, it is a free gift. We began with the fundamental affirmation that every human being is a unique and mysterious gift. This giftedness is seen both in our birth and in our baptism. By *mysterious*, we do not mean odd or weird. We mean that, when everything has been said about a person, something beyond words is still there that simply will not yield to explanation.

Christianity, when it is true to itself, seeks to foster the unfolding of individuals and of communities *as mysteries.* It is unashamedly affirmative in claiming that the root cause of human mystery is the inexhaustible mystery of God. This, for us, is Christian doctrine: something to be believed. Because Christianity is concerned with human wholeness, this doctrine (that human beings are mysteries) is not so much an intellectual assertion as a call to adventure. There is no possibility of our somehow exploring our own mystery as spectators. We can not be mere onlookers. We are actors in our own drama.

How do we know what it is to be fully human? How do we know what a truly human community is? The Christian knows only one answer: the model of Jesus Christ. Christ is absolutely central as the one who not only opens up the way to our becoming full human beings but also is himself the

Way. Indeed, one great Christian defined Christianity as the manifestation of God, and the summons to Personality.[1]

To Be Christian Is to Be Fully Human

Christianity is a call to be fully human, and the full manifestation of *personality* would have to be human just like us. It would have to appear in our flesh, with all the limitations of space and time. So when we insist on the centrality of Christ (the One who manifests what it is to be a person and what it is to be a people), we are saying two things about human beings. The first is that our life is God-centered, that there is the gracious and loving *otherness* at the center of our lives. The second thing we are saying is that this God-centeredness is firmly rooted in the material world, in the ordinary, and in the routine things of life. Christ shows us what it is to be a person, and a person is not a disembodied spirit.

Who we are, then, and who we are becoming is bound up with the person of Jesus. But Christ is not a model in the sense that we are to be exactly like him in every respect. To do this we would not only have to think like a man in Palestine of the first century (which, in fact, is impossible for us), we would also all have to be male! No, when we say that Jesus Christ is the model of what we are to become, we mean that though the redemptive power of his life we become what we are meant to be—a unique unrepeatable manifestation of what it is to be human.

As we enter more deeply into our own mystery, we discover a strange double truth about our growing and developing as human beings: The first, as we have seen, is that human existence, even understood as sheer survival, as a pattern of personal relationships, as a quest for integrity and wholeness, is a gift. The second is that our development and growth as human beings is also a challenge, a task, a job to be done. Human living is not only a gift, it is also an achievement. The gift demands our acceptance in faith and commitment; the task, our disciplined and loving attention.

We are challenged then with gift and task, with commitment and discipline: commitment in faith to a vision of reality; discipline in following that vision as honestly and as courageously as we can. We have, as it were, been given equipment for an immense journey, and now we feel that it is time to begin the adventure into new and untrod ways. Indeed we have already begun it. We were thrust into it at our birth and at our baptism. We now come to the practical application of what we believe in every waking moment. What does it mean to practice to be a disciple of Jesus Christ?

Christian Discipleship

Christian discipleship is concerned with the various ways in which we seek to live out the implications of our faith in Christ on both a personal and a communal level. What difference does this commitment make in ordinary little ways? Does our faith reach deep down into the trivial and commonplace as well as into the important and extraordinary? Christian spirituality has to do with both the ordinary and the extraordinary in human life.

The methods we employ in living out our faith traditionally come under the heading of *ascetics*. *Ascesis* is simply the Greek word for exercise (particularly of an athlete). It has come to mean a discipline undertaken by a person to achieve a certain end: The athlete, the musician, and the actor go through a regime of routines and exercises in order to be able to give of their very best. In fact, the simplest things we take for granted, earning a living, cooking, gardening, making ends meet, all require effort, concentration, and discipline. Ascetics is also a word that suggests, to some, hard and intolerable disciplines like those of the hollow-cheeked monks who stood up to their necks in ice-cold water with their arms outstretched (although, to be fair, some of them were indeed great saints). Worse than that, Christian discipline suggests sets of rules and regulations by which we can, somehow, make ourselves worthy of God's love. Nothing could be further from the heart of the Gospel. There are no first- and second-class citizens in the Kingdom of God, and our salvation does not depend on our performing certain rituals or undergoing rigorous acts of discipline. We cannot earn God's love any more than our newborn baby can earn his parents' love.

The first principle in guiding us on the road to becoming human is this: *All is gift and the gift that God gives us is himself*. God gives us himself in so many different ways, and our relationship to him is rich and varied.

Images and Metaphors for Becoming Human

Pictures and images are very important because they help us get under the skin of things. They are the means by which we penetrate places too deep for ordinary language. They come to our aid in asking such questions as: Who is this baby who is born and then reborn? How does he become who and what he is? How does Christian spirituality help us understand the mystery of human personality? A spirituality firmly grounded in the down-to-earth (that is what we mean by *incarnational*), which is also fundamentally God-centered, provides us with some metaphors for becoming human— metaphors that are rooted in the common heritage of Jews and Christians. There are, for example, the metaphors of election (being chosen), of conversion (making a new beginning), of maturity (growing up), and of transformation into community (becoming a people).

ELECTION: BEING CHOSEN

"How odd of God to choose the Jews!" Many of us learned this tag in the early years of our schooling. It sprang, perhaps, from an unconscious anti-Semitism, and deeper still, from a certain jealousy. Doesn't the very idea of a chosen people imply that God is unfair, that he has favorites? Why should God choose somebody else and not me? This wonderful gift of election, however, was not conferred on the ancient Israelites for their exclusive possession, nor was it given in order to make things easier for them than for other people. It was not a set of privileges conferred by membership in an exclusive club. On the contrary, it was given to them to be broken open and shared out like bread with all the world. The calling of the chosen is to be *for* the not-yet-chosen. The elect of God are a sign that God chooses us all.

The prophet Amos points to the cost of this call:

> You only have I known
> > of all the families of the earth;
> therefore . . . (Amos 3:2)

Therefore what? I will go easy on you? I will gloss over your offenses? Not at all. Because you are my chosen, you are to be holy for the sake of others.

> > therefore I will punish you
> > > for all your iniquities (Amos 3:2).

This is a very strange *therefore* and difficult for us to understand. Another prophet (sometimes referred to as the third Isaiah) describes the final working-out of being chosen in these terms:

> I am coming to gather all nations and tongues; and they shall come and shall see my glory . . . . Some of them also I will take for priests and for Levites, says the Lord (Is. 66:18b, 21).

In the end, God chooses all peoples through the one chosen people. No one is left outside.

CONVERSION: MAKING A NEW BEGINNING

Another metaphor for becoming human is the word *conversion*. It means turning, and we hear it again and again in Scripture. "Turn, turn, turn," says the Lord, "turn to me and be radiant" (Ps. 80:3).[2] "Unless you turn and become little children you will never enter the Kingdom of heaven" (Mt. 18:3). The word itself suggests that something has gone wrong, that we have lost our way, taken a wrong path, and are either wandering aimlessly or progressing rapidly towards a mistaken goal, towards disaster.

Turning is a very simple act, simpler than swimming

against the current or cutting a path through briars. It is a matter of taking a different attitude towards someone, or something, of letting down one's guard, or of giving up a judgmental point of view. For Christians, it is turning from trust in power, or status, or a sense of one's own consistency and rectitude, towards trust in a mercy and goodness beyond our own. This turning (even if it's only a small movement) involves a shift of our vision so that, in a sense, everything changes: the way we look at the world, at others, at ourselves, and at the things we think matter. To turn and to live in response to the call and choice of our Maker is to be human.

MATURITY: GROWING UP

The word *maturity* has a contemporary sound; but in the letter to the Ephesians being a mature human being is equated with "the measure of the stature of the fullness of Christ." This is the key to our understanding of maturity. It is wholeness in Christ and in his members. Many of us have experienced the healing power of certain personalities. Just being with them makes us feel more open, more loving, and more real. They have the power of making things whole, of drawing us to a fuller maturity. This is the power of the person of Christ. Healing personalities give us a glimpse of the transforming power of Christ.

Maturity, like election, doesn't imply a privileged position with regard to the *immature*. Some people grow more rapidly than others towards fullness in Christ, not in order to form a kind of spiritual life but to be signs of what we are all called to become. This growth in maturity actually draws us all closer together in community. For this development isn't so much a matter of the individual growing in isolation as it is a situation where we concentrate on a center outside ourselves. We are like the spokes of a great wheel: The closer we get to the center the closer we are to one another. The center, for us, is Christ. That is why Christian maturity focuses our attention upon the oneness of the body of Christ, the community into which we are called and into which we enter by Baptism, "for we are members one of another." So being mature, being human, involves finding a place and a meaning in relationships with others.

The meaning of being human is a mystery because it is both obscure and deep. They are not the same thing. The word *obscure* can mean two things. It can mean that something is hidden from us in some dark place, or it can describe something that is lost, so lost that it has no meaning. Obscurity, in this latter sense, is the result of our lostness, our fragmentation, and our being turned the wrong way. But men and women are mysteries in another way also. The meaning and the unity of human life are so deep and so high that they go beyond our understanding.

There is an important distinction to be made between a problem and a mystery. A problem is something that can, in principle, be solved; and when it is solved, it no longer exists. A mystery, on the other hand, is something that can be penetrated more and more and that yields an even deeper, more complex, and wonderful meaning that can never be exhausted. Hence, mystery remains. Human life is a mystery. It is not a problem. Maturity, therefore, is seeing life as a mystery, not as a problem.

BECOMING A PEOPLE: THE STORY OF THE PEOPLE OF GOD

One of the ways in which people have explored the meaning of their own mystery is recorded for us in the Bible. The Old Testament is the story of how the Israelites became the people of God, how they understood their own experience. It is the interpretation of this story that is important. People are flesh and blood. They are made in time and space. That is why history is so important. It is the record of the making of peoples. As secular history goes, the events recorded in the Bible are relatively insignificant. They concern a wandering Semitic people, one group among many others; and except for the extraordinary fact of their being chosen and their response to it, they seem to have been singularly ungifted. The general pattern of their story is one of going down and coming up. They went down into Egypt, a place of false worship and of false power, and they came up through the watery mud of the Sea of Reeds (the Red Sea), through the desert of Sinai , and into the ploughed land—the land called Canaan. Here, after a bloody conquest, they built the temple where alone the one true God could be worshiped. The God whom they worshiped was the bringing-out-of-Egypt God, the deliverer.

When we consider the story in more detail we can see that going down into Egypt and coming up through the desert was more than an experience of deliverance. Something happened in the darkness of Egypt and in the spiritual darkness and temptation of the wilderness journey, something that transformed the Jews from a loose nomadic band into a new community, the covenant people of God.

How this transformation took place is recorded in the Bible by means of dramatic images: a bit of desert scrub suddenly blazing up in flames without charring the wood as the sign of Moses' call to lead his people out of Egypt; the escape of the Hebrew slaves and the drowning of the soldiers of Pharaoh in the sea; the smoking mountain and the lightning and thunder that Moses entered alone, as representative of his people, before Yahweh. All of these images signify the patient and unrelenting pursuit of the Lord, seeking to win to himself the hearts of the people he had chosen. In that turning they were changed. The tablets of stone and the solemn covenant between Yahweh and Israel, sealed in the blood of sacrifice, were signs of a new creation, of a people bound to God by the covenant. This covenant, initiated by the Lord, bound the children of Israel to God. They were his people. He was their God. It was a demanding covenant that expected an exclusive loyalty and obedience on the part of Israel. God, in his turn, would love and protect his people. To *be* Israel was to be bound to God in a covenant relationship.

God and Israel were not equal partners. The relationship between them was not one of mutuality. Israel's part in the covenant was the acceptance of Yahweh as their God. The Ten Commandments were a summary of their obligations to him. Yahweh, for his part, promised to be their God, and he revealed himself to them as their deliverer, able and willing to save them from a hopeless situation, and looking upon them with merciful love. This love never changed, however badly they behaved, because merciful preserving love is at the heart of God's reality.

The people of Israel had only to keep in their minds the great deliverance from Egypt, the Exodus, to realize just how much God loved them. Deliverance here is more than just being pulled out of a terrible pit or extracted from a trap. It refers also to the experience of transformation, of change and renewal, which happens in the helplessness and darkness of the trap and the pit. Out of the very fact of being trapped and lost in the dark comes the promise of new life, comes deliverance.

If we look back, each of us, upon our own lives, we can see the same pattern. Our story is the story of going down and coming up. In fact we say that life has its ups and downs. To be sure, these heights and depths are hardly as dramatic as the great Exodus. Nevertheless, certain events, an illness, a death in the family, a colossal disappointment, can be shattering experiences that act as a prelude to our transformation.

The New Covenant Written on the Heart

The covenant people of God entered the promised land, built a temple to worship in, and made a record of the revealed will of God for his people, the commandments preserved in the Ark and enshrined in the Holy Place. Unfortunately, this is not the end of the story. As prophet after prophet tells us, they neither remained faithful in their worship of the one and only God, nor did they obey his will as it was expressed in their sacred writings. They worshiped false gods, not only foreign deities, not-gods, and demons, but they also worshiped power, possessions, and pleasure. God was tired of the whole business, and he did two things about it. He allowed the Chaldeans to destroy Jerusalem, and he determined to make a fresh start with his people. The Prophet

Jeremiah (31:31–34) tells us that God determined to make a new covenant not like the old covenant "which they broke, though I was their husband." The new covenant would not be written on tablets. It would be interior: "I will write it upon their hearts."

When we look at Israel after the fall of Jerusalem, we see a people weakened and humiliated by their defeat, and confused by the apparent failure of God's promises. Jeremiah had said that "David shall never lack a man to sit on the throne of the house of Israel" (Jer. 33:17). This prophecy was fulfilled, not by the restoration of the line of David to the throne of Israel, but by the coming of a very different kind of king, Jesus of Nazareth.

This covenant of the heart, this wonderful alliance between God and his people, is sealed for us in Jesus Christ. He is the sign that God and humanity belong to one another. In him God and the human race are so bound together, so covenanted, that they will never be parted.

The Christian mystery of the Incarnation (God showing himself in the flesh) means that the heart of one man, Jesus of Nazareth, was so at one with the will of his Father that his whole chosen, conscious, and costing life became the *new* covenant. Into this covenant and this kingdom we are born in our baptism. We understand the mystery of our own life in the light of the story of this man, Jesus.

· 3 ·

A Human Being
Is the Image of God

The mystery of being human is referred to in manuals of theology as *the doctrine of man*. Although the use of the word *man* is generic here, as is clear in the original language of the Old Testament, it cannot be overemphasized that women as well as men are made in the image of God. "So God created man in his own image, in the image of God he created him; male and female he created them."

There are two creation stories in the Bible (the first in Genesis 1:27, the second in Genesis 2:2–22). Although these two stories are found in the first two chapters of the first book of the Bible, they were actually written long after the events of the Exodus, and they are best understood as the insights of the people of God looking back, through the story of their deliverance and their entrance into the covenant. They looked back over the stories of their ancestors, the patriarchs, and wrote about the mystery of human beginnings. The creation stories are attempts at answering the question: "Where did humanity come from?" This is not so very different from what we do all the time. If, for example, you wanted to describe your own beginnings to someone (say you wanted to describe your home life when you were three years old) you would tell your story from the perspective of all the intervening years. You would interpret, you would explain in the light of what happened later. Imagine what it would be like to try to describe the beginnings of the human race!

It is very hard for us to imagine our own beginnings, let alone the beginning of the whole human adventure. How does one describe sight to one who has never seen? How are we to understand the mystery of creation itself? Why, we may ask, is there anything at all, and not just nothing? The writers of the book of Genesis were faced with the mystery of our beginnings. They wrote a wonderful story to illuminate their questions. They talked about the *otherness* within, in story form. This *otherness* was called *the image of God.*

How can we think about the dramatic change from the formlessness, emptiness, and nothingness before creation, to the wonderful reality of concrete separate beings? The Biblical images give us bridges, metaphors by which to make this unimaginable leap.

> The Spirit of God was moving over the face of the waters. And God said, 'Let there be light'; and there was light (Gen. 1:2b, 3b).

> Then the Lord God formed man of dust from the ground, and breathed into his nostrils the breath of life, and man became a living being (Gen. 2:7).

In the New Testament, the fourth Gospel begins with another imaginative statement about beginnings:

> In the beginning was the Word, and the Word was with God, and the Word was God. He was in the beginning with God; all things were made through him, and without him was not anything made that was made. In him was life, and the life was the light of men (Jn. 1:1–4).

> But to all who received him, who believed in his name, he gave power to become children of God (Jn. 1:12).

This tells us something more about the identity of the child who has been born and then reborn. All things, including the newborn baby, were made through the word of God. Everything owes its being to him, and in him everything finds its true fulfillment. It is Christ, the word of God, through whom the child was made, who reveals to us the meaning of being human.

To be made after the divine image means that we share in God's life. To share in God's life is to share in mystery. But so much of who God is, is hidden from us because we are finite and mortal. So much of what we are is also hidden from us since we find our being in the mystery of God. We too then are hidden from ourselves. Why? Because "It doth not yet appear what we shall be."

The unfinished, incomplete character of human beings is the occasion of both crisis and opportunity: crisis, because we feel insecure when we are faced with the open and unknown; opportunity, because only in the open and in the unknown is new life. The hunger for relationship, for intimacy, for a life shared with others, is inevitably linked to its deadly opposite: the fear of loneliness, of emptiness, of meaninglessness. As we grow in the Christian life, we learn that genuine intimacy is given only to those who have learned to live creatively within their own solitude. As the poet Marianne Moore put it: "The only cure for loneliness is solitude." It is in solitude that the image of God comes alive in us, that the *otherness* of the Holy Spirit has its way with us.

The Power of Silence

The accumulated wisdom of centuries teaches us that God speaks to the human heart most intimately only in silence. Silence and an inner emptiness or receptivity are the strange conditions for all our relationships. Without the ability to be silent, to wait, to be receptive, all our attempts at communion become manipulative and possessive. We become frustrated because we want instant gratification. We want all of who we are to be revealed. We want to know the end of the story. We find it difficult to wait. Waiting in the stillness is, perhaps, the hardest of all human activities. It is not only hard. It is dangerous. The act of self-emptying leaves us open to attack from other quarters. Jesus himself warns us about this:

> When the unclean spirit has gone out of a man, he passes through waterless places seeking rest; and finding none he says, "I will return to my house from which I came." And when he comes he finds it swept and put in order. Then he goes and brings seven other spirits more evil than himself, and they enter and dwell there; and the last state of that man becomes worse than the first (Lk. 11:24–26).

Yet it is only in silence that who we really are (the true image) begins to appear. In the end we need not fear, for it is our own best self struggling within, longing to be free.

The Covenant Story Is Our Story

The story of the covenant people is very much our own story. It is not distant or remote. We can understand our own lives in terms of falling and of rising. There are many stories about how human beings fall down in the Bible. They fall as individuals, and Israel falls as a nation. It is not difficult to see ourselves and the affairs of the world in each one: in Adam and in Eve, in Sarah laughing at God, and in Abraham being less than honest, in David taking the wife of Uriah, and in the kings and queens of Israel and Judah who "did that which was evil in the sight of the Lord."

The fall of Jerusalem is a very powerful image of our own falls. Jerusalem was the Holy City, the place where God dwelt. Its fall is the sign that even the most sacred and most sure, even the place of the reign of God on earth, can be shattered. Sometimes it is our religion, so often a place of privilege and protection, that needs to be broken open by what appears at the time to be a terrible fall. It was only after the collapse of all that was most holy, including the law itself, that the promise of the new covenant was made to Jeremiah. Henceforth the people of God looked forward to a new deliverance and a new Exodus. A faithful remnant waited in patience, penitence, and humility for a future kingdom that they could not even imagine. They could only hope.

So it is with us. We get comfortable and secure in our religion. We treat it like an old coat in the closet that we can drag out on cold winter mornings. It's there if we need it, in an emergency. It isn't the mainspring of life. We domesticate Christianity and take away its demanding bite. Then our *Jerusalem* falls. The bottom falls out of our world, and out of the rubble, a Jeremiah speaks to us again and again of a new beginning, a new hope. As we shall see, the life of prayer has such ups and downs.

The period after the fall of Jerusalem and the end of the Judean kingdom was a time of national defeat from which, on the historical level, the people of Israel were never to recover. There never was a successor to the last Davidic king. Palestine was occupied by foreign rulers, and gradually some of the inhabitants rose to positions of relative power only through collaboration with the enemy. This involved not only working with the occupying force but accepting his gods as well. Those who wished to prosper compromised. A second group of people gradually sank into the lowest social rank. These were the noncollaborators who remained faithful to the worship of the God of Israel. They are the "poor of God," of whom we hear in the first two chapters of Luke: Elizabeth and Zachariah, Mary, a virgin betrothed to Joseph, Simeon, and Anna.

Simeon, who was called "righteous and devout," looking for the consolation of Israel, recognized the promised Messiah in the child Jesus who was brought to him in the temple. He understood him to be a savior not only for Israel, but in accordance with the prophecy of Isaiah, a savior of the nations, of the whole world.

It was to Mary that the invitation was given to become the mother of Jesus the Christ, the promised deliverer. It is to this woman with empty hands that God gives the son to be a new beginning for the human race. Just as we can discern in the history of the chosen people a pattern of falling and rising, so in the life of Jesus we see the same pattern; and his pattern is ours. He came down, "emptied himself, taking the form of a servant, being born in the likeness of men" (Phil. 2:7). He lived a fully human life, sharing our experience of dependent childhood, obedience, and apprenticeship. Then, at the moment of his baptism, his vocation as Messiah was revealed to him.

The Christian's Call to Prayer

What Christ accomplished on the Cross, *once and for all*, in a particular place at a particular time, is now the source of all our being and doing. The Christian's call to discipleship in prayer is a call to share in the whole life of the Lord, in his dying and in his rising. We are not only to bear our Cross, but, strangely, to bear also the Resurrection. In the Gospels the accounts of the call of the disciples resembles the Old Testament accounts of the call of the prophets. We are called in this manner, too. We read accounts of individual experiences summoning a person to leave familiar tasks and well-trod paths behind, and to explore new ways, ways that involve risk and call for strength far beyond their powers. The response to the call itself is an experience of transformation. Christians are called to take up the cross and follow. As we hear this word in faith and open ourselves to receive the gift hidden in the call, we are taken up into life on a different level, the level of what the New Testament calls the Kingdom. The life of prayer is largely a waiting in patience for the call, a quiet and intense listening for the creative word that proclaims the reign of God.

The Call to Community

The church in Jerusalem, of which Luke gives us a description in the Book of Acts, understood this call in terms of community. Our vocation to discipleship is understood as a call to a common life and a common unity, in the apostles' teaching and fellowship, the breaking of bread, and the prayers (Acts 2:42).

> And all who believed were together and had all things in common; and they sold their possessions and goods and distributed them to all, as any had need (Acts 2:44–45).

The spiritual life is a shared life and is patterned after the central New Testament image of the Cross and the Resurrection of Christ. This pattern of dying and rising, the ups and downs of all our relationships, follows and shares the pattern of Christ's dying and rising. At the heart of our experience of darkness and failure, the Holy Spirit gives new life.

The Voice of Experience

It seems to me that every good thing I ever tried to do for God and his Kingdom brought me sooner or later into humiliation and despair. I reached the end of my capacities and my vision all too soon, and could carry nothing through to fruition. My best intentions irritated other people and set up centers of resistance and opposition in them, which threatened to defeat the whole project. Sometimes that was the end of it. Perhaps I had misconceived my powers, my possibilities, and the will of God for me, and was setting out towards an illusory goal, a little fantasy of my own. Perhaps I gave up too soon. Whatever the cause, I have come to recognize the inevitable bankruptcy of my trying to play the role of God even in a modest way of trying to organize and control my little world. When obstacles arise before my eyes and black pits open in the path before my feet, sometimes I just stop there.

Other times, however, by an act of faith, I go on, down into the darkness of the situation, where I have to confront the reality of my sin, my pride, and my exaggeration. I have to look at my cowardice and at my refusal of love. I also know, both from the witness of Scripture and the experience of many Christians through the ages, that my experience is far from unique. Such setbacks and confrontations are common. These conflicts can bring us, just as we are, prideful, deluded, frail, and cowardly, into the circle of the Holy Cross, into the sphere of transformation. There we discover that the place of ultimate despair has another face. The discovery is like getting up out of bed one morning, after a long night of struggle and suffering, and realizing that the conflict is over and the victory is won, and not by us. It is given. Moreover, that which is given is not just restored relationships with the pieces put back together as they were before, but a new creation, a different perspective, and a fresh beginning. The sun has risen upon a new day.

This is a personal witness of renewal and transformation, when, by the grace of God, everything is bathed in new light. This kind of event is often sudden and dramatic. It comes to us as sheer gift: out of the blue. There are other ways of understanding renewal and conversion that are no less dramatic but are slow and gradual. They are evolutionary rather than revolutionary.

· 4 ·

Becoming Human
Is a Pilgrimage

Some of the most ancient metaphors for the spiritual life have to do with journeys. One of the best known of these is that of Abraham. He is the ancestor of the faith in one God that Christians share with both Jews and Arabs.

God revealed himself to Abraham by calling him out, away from the familiar succession of grazing grounds, caravan routes, and comforting family gatherings on the edge of cities, to go northward towards an unknown destination. The goal of his journey was hidden from him. He had no idea where his response to God would lead him. His ready obedience to this call makes him a model of faith for us today.

The Pilgrim Fathers of American history were also called, as they understood it, to leave everything they knew and, in obedience to God whom they could not worship freely at home, to set forth, in faith, to an unknown destination.

In medieval times the faithful set out on another kind of journey, a pilgrimage, often through unknown and danger-ous country, towards a *known* destination: the shrine of a saint, for example, that of Thomas à Becket at Canterbury, or of St. James of Compostella in Spain. Pilgrims still go to such places as the Holy Land, or to a place where miracles happen—Lourdes, for instance.

Entering the Desert

Early Christian writers understood the Christian life as a desert journey, and took for its model that mighty event that was explored in the last chapter, the Exodus and the forty years the children of Israel spent crossing the desert between Sinai and the Promised Land.

The image of the desert in Scripture is a double one. Literally, it means an uninhabited waste place without water or shelter. Deserts were thought to be inhabited by evil spirits of all sorts and were known, therefore, as places of temptation. The temptation of Jesus took place in the desert, and the first monks understood their vocation as a call out of a common life in a cultivated land to do battle with demons in the wilderness.

The desert was also a place of vision, of innocence, and of meeting with God. The prophets thought of this wandering in the wilderness as the time in Israel's life when she was faithful to God. Desert life, as it is described in the Exodus, was a life of great simplicity, free from corruption and luxury, where the Hebrews were dependent upon the daily and nightly manifestation of God's presence—the pillar of cloud by day and the pillar of fire at night. It was also the place where they received food and drink from the hand of God himself, the manna in the wilderness and the water from the rock. The desert, from this point of view, is a place of transformation, a sort of golden age, when God and his people were very close to one another.

In early Christian literature the theme of struggle, combat, and progress in the desert are combined with the apparently opposite theme of visitation and contemplation. The Christian life was understood as both struggle and contemplation. Life in the Spirit was seen as a progress upwards, an ascent that might lead into heaven itself. Spirituality (becoming human) was a task. Books by the monks presented the Christian life in terms of a struggle upwards. It often became a striving to reach God. One got to God by slow degrees, by the arduous climbing of steps and ladders. This has its good side. Becoming fully human is a task, but if we concentrate on this too much we lose sight of the most important thing of all: Becoming human is also a free gift.

The Two Ways: Imitation and Penetration

In these early books, progress was seen in two ways: the first as the literal following of Jesus Christ, like that of St. Francis of Assisi, and second, as a process of the interior penetration of the heart by the Spirit of Christ. In the first way, we have a spirituality based on meditation on the life of Christ and on our efforts to reproduce that life in our actual experience. Christ, as it were, comes alive in us when we try to imitate him. The other way takes the Christian journey through the desert and understands it as an interior pilgrimage. It makes the spiritual life a progressive transformation of the whole of life with the vision of God as its goal. To be sure one cannot entirely separate these two ways. It is really a question of emphasis.

The journey is a very useful model, but unless it is related to the theme of being transformed into the likeness of Christ its usefulness is limited. The Christian life is not a journey with everything neatly mapped out and where the destination is within easy reach. It simply is not within our power to arrive at our goal through our own efforts. The Kingdom of God is not earned or achieved; it is inherited. That is to say, it is given to us. As we have seen, we enter it by baptism. We seek the goal and strive to get there, but in the end we do not progress in a straight line. Much of our journeying actually gets us nowhere. Far from going in a straight line, we are like a plane in a holding pattern over an airport, waiting for a space to land. Much of our life appears to be such a holding pattern.

One way, one journey emphasizes our need to imitate Christ, to be like him; the other way, our need to allow him to enter into our life and transform it.

When we think about the spiritual life as moving with great difficulty through the desert, the place of demons, we conceive of faithfulness in terms of resistance, hard work, and discipline. When we think of it, on the other hand, in terms of transformation, we use different words. Progress in this instance is seen as a gift that recreates and renews us. The goal is communion with God in the life of prayer. There has always been tension between these two ideals, of active discipline and of contemplation, although the two live together in each one of us. This same tension between the spiritual life as gift and as task is seen in the theological themes that underlie the two ways of viewing the Christian life.

There is the doctrine that the image of God is in every one of us, down somewhere at the bottom of our being but hidden under layers of defilement. This defilement was thought of in concrete terms as mud or clay, rust or stain, and it was believed that the task of the Christian life was to scrape off these layers of dirt and discover the image within. This is the ascetic way: the way of hard work.

A different way of regarding the Christian life, less dependent upon a low view of human beings and of the material world, gave a central place to the fact that God himself took away the defilement. He scraped off the layers of dirt. Conversion is the lightning flash of insight that enables us to see what God has done for us. In this view, life in Christ is a gift, "tossed in from without, like a burning brand."

Various efforts have been made to bring these two ways of thinking into a relationship. It is obvious that each has its truth and its importance, but it is not so easy to reconcile them. One way of doing so is to consider, as the Protestant Reformers tended to do, that the hard work is the sign of justification and not the preparation for it, far less the cause of it. Another attempt at reconciliation produced a distinction between two kinds of faith, *unformed faith* referred to in the Epistle of James as the faith of "devils who believe and tremble." Another example would be the faith of Augustine, who prayed for grace to change his life, that is, for repentance, "But not yet!" He was convinced of the truth of the Catholic faith, but wanted a little time before he took the yoke of Christ upon him. His faith was *unformed*. The other kind of faith was called *faith formed by charity*. This is saving faith; the faith that is alive and fruitful. It brings forth acts of love, because that is its nature. Discipline undertaken for the sake of love is therefore a part of saving faith.

The Life of Prayer: The Longing to Be Known

The quest for healing, wholeness, and holiness brings millions of widely differing human beings together in a common cause. Men and women in business, in research, in everyday jobs, in homes for the dying, in places where a newborn child utters its first cry, all share common questions. "Do I matter?" "How should I live?" "What happens when I die?" "Does anyone care?" The Christian life of prayer is the means by which we plumb the depths of these questions and live the questions out in our everyday lives. Prayer is the spontaneous response to God from these inner depths. The pilgrimage through these interior places is not always easy. When we come up against difficulties, we are tempted to by-pass them or seek easy answers.

PRAYER IS THE WAY OF LOVE

Prayer is the way through our human clumsiness and insensitivity. We long to be loved just as we are. But we have to be still, be silent, wait, and allow ourselves time to be loved. Human help, however warm and deep, has its limits. St. Augustine's words express a universal truth: "Thou hast made us for thyself and our heart is restless until it rest in Thee." People long for a love that accepts them, "warts and all." And prayer, if it is honest, exposes everything that we are with no pretense. A love that requires drastic cosmetic surgery so that we can hide all blemishes and appear with a surface beauty is no love at all. Christian prayer is the way of love. It is a way of self-surrender. Friends, loved ones, therapists, and clergy can help us discover that self that has to be surrendered in love. This is not self-rejection. And it is not self-fulfillment in the shallow terms of our acquisitive society.

Christian self-surrender in prayer is the act of taking ourselves out of our own hands and placing ourselves, just as we are, in the hands of God. In this way, we live out our baptism when we were taken from the hands of our parents and sponsors and placed in the expansive and loving hands of God.

The Christian pilgrimage is not the way of self-rejection nor (in the popular sense) of self-fulfillment. Our self-surrender is to the Holy Spirit who continually invites us to go beyond what we know of ourselves. It's as if he said to us: "There's so much more to you than that splinter, that tiny fragment you call yourself. Give that tiny thing up and come with me. You are much more than you ever dreamed." The Holy Spirit invites us to go on a pilgrimage of exploration into the mystery of God himself in all his inexhaustible wonder.

The adventure of interior exploration, however, requires self-emptying. As we have seen, the children of Israel had to do this. They had to be *emptied* of their life in Egypt. They had to journey into the wilderness to meet God.

This is the way God comes to us when we have begun to let go. That old phrase, "Let go and let God!" has a great deal of truth in it. Everything is to be surrendered, not to deprive us of the things we hold dear, but so we may receive them again at the Lord's hand. We are invited to surrender both heart and mind: to empty both and wait for them to be filled.

PRAYER IS THE LIFE OF THE MIND

The emptying of the mind has left Christians open to the criticism that they do not value their intellect. Christianity, however, at its center, is neither anti-intellectual nor irrational. There is an old saying, "Only two things will save the world: thought and prayer. The trouble is that people who think don't pray and the people who pray don't think!" Christian spirituality, focused as it is on the wholeness of men and women, is concerned with the life of the mind as well as of the will and the emotions. Spirituality seeks to live out a marriage of thought and prayer. It encourages as full and vigorous a mental life as is possible for each individual. We are to use our minds to the full. We use our minds in reflecting on our everyday experience of the world.

God comes to us through the things he has made, especially our fellow human beings. We must also remember that God is the creator of our thinking and the architect of human events. Thoughts and happenings are his creatures too, and he speaks to us through them. Everything we experience, the good and the bad, can be the means by which God reaches us. We shape and are shaped by our experiences. It is the mind that enables us to interpret experiences, but if the mind is not open to the Holy Spirit, we misinterpret them. We may succumb to the illusion that we actually created the experiences. This misinterpretation often causes us to concentrate on an experience as if it were our own prized possession. We get stuck. Or we might have an important experience that changes our life. But if we're not careful, we might easily get stuck in that experience and become immobilized. Or we long for a single experience that will solve all our problems.

True prayer does not allow for wishful thinking. It takes us out of ourselves, out of our concerns, even out of our hopes and longings (our little Egypts), and puts us in a still, quiet place to wait for God. Courage to make our own Exodus is given us by our sharing in common human experiences.

Everything we experience enters into us. The bird-watcher watching his birds, the fisherman catching fish, and the businessman at work are not merely studying birds, fish, and business. They are also exploring themselves. When you plan to do anything: cook dinner, go to a movie, read a book, you are not only doing something *out there,* you are also, somehow, expressing what is going on *inside* you. When you discover something new, you discover something new about yourself. All knowledge is, in some sense, self-knowledge. Things have an *inwardness* about them. There is no world totally *out there.* But neither is there a world that is totally inward. The inner and the outer worlds are, in reality, one. It is this connection between inner and outer realities that is the concern of Christian spirituality. The pilgrimage upon which we are embarked involves the skillful making of creative connections between the two great worlds in which we live—the inner and the outer.

Prayer is discovering the loving and creative connections between the world within and the world outside us. It demands the double commitment of creative thinking and of outgoing love.

Pilgrimage as Transformation

Our journey towards God involves stepping stones. These steps not only lead towards a goal but often represent moments of transformation. An important stepping-stone experience, for example, can remake us from top to bottom. It gives us a new vision of ourselves and the world. When we make these steps in faith, there is a surge of new life. It's like being in love, everything looks different. That is why prayer and contemplation are at the heart of the converted life. Contemplation is simply seeing or gazing at what we believe to be the real.

Try making a list of your *stepping stones*. They do not have to be particularly dramatic or even especially religious. Simply write down those turning points in your life that were important to you. They may be experiences that welled up from inside, or were forced upon you from outside: the year when you were six years old and you moved from Katonah, New York, to Pasadena, California; the car accident you had in the first year of your marriage; the first trip you took away from home; the time you lost your job; the time when you first said "yes" to Christ. Think about these turning points and dwell on them as places where the Holy Spirit was present.

It is our covenant relationship with God that gives our pilgrimage direction and hope. Our relationship with God is not unlike those we have with our fellow human beings. There are things there too that we do not understand. There are moments we would prefer to forget. There are those memories that cause us pain, and those that we treasure. It is, in the end, the relationship that is important. Christian prayer is basically dwelling in our fundamental covenant relationship with God. It is not primarily a dwelling on what we consider our failures and achievements in that relationship. We are who we are because he is who he is. Only in a secondary sense are we who we are because of what we have done.

This covenant relationship we have with God frees us from the burden of self-concern. We don't have to worry about our image, whether it be high or low. This is what it means to be born of the Spirit. Contemplation, which is the long, loving gaze at God, is at the heart of this freedom. In our contemplative moments, we are given a sense of meaning and purpose. The great Covenant is not so much something to strive for; it is, rather, something that is already given. It has only to be accepted.

What Christ has done *for us* on the Cross, he must be allowed to do *in us*. Bethlehem, Calvary, and Resurrection become the transforming inner events in the life of the Spirit in a movement toward healing and wholeness.

For some of us, a place has special significance in our spiritual histories. Places are important reminders of our stepping stones, and we can in our prayer-time return to such places. Imagine a small chapel in a large church in the north of England. It is very early in the morning. There is one ray of rising sun shining through the window behind the altar. It is very still. The austere lines of the Norman architecture, the cold stone, the flickering light before the blessed sacrament. This beautiful little chapel might hold for you a remembrance of conversion, a symbol of transformation. You will know such places, and it is good, from time to time, to go back and recapture a special moment of turning.

There are significant stepping stones not only for individuals but also for families, institutions, and nations. These too can be entered into imaginatively in order to try to understand what God was doing in these events. Things that seemed destructive and disastrous when they happened look different ten years later. We often see a great good working itself out of what appeared at the time to be an awful episode. The reverse is true, too. There are turns for the worse. What appeared to be a constructive and good thing can be seen as exactly the opposite in the course of time.

What we learn from our Christian commitment is that whatever has happened to us (the joys and the tragedies, the successes and the failures) can be used by God for our deeper transformation. All that has ever happened to us can be used, even the moments of darkness, because there is absolutely nothing beyond the reach of God. St. Paul affirmed:

We know that in everything God works for good with those who love him, who are called according to His purpose (Rom. 8:28).

· 5 ·

The Road to Wholeness

We have just thought about the stepping stones that punctuate our lives. The question is, do they lead anywhere? Are we going someplace? We know that turning (conversion) is a very important part of our growth as humans, but to whom are we to turn in order to live a more fully human life? We not only believe that the stepping stones lead us *to* God, but also that he is *with* us every step of the way.

At its heart Christianity proclaims that the goal of human life is nothing less than God himself. This is the glorious news of our salvation: We are destined to share in the life of God. At our baptism we are taken into this new life. Our baptism is a proclamation that we belong, that we have a family. One way of expressing this is to say that we are *members* of Christ. To be a member (that is, a limb) of Christ is to share in a life that is not our own, and to be joined to the other members as intimately as the various parts of the human body are held together. This intimacy has an important part to play in our praying, since we are always praying within the fellowship of those who are *in Christ*. In other words, we are never alone, even in our solitude, because in Christ we are members one of another; we belong to one great family.

The human community is meant to be as closely knit and as harmoniously proportioned as the human body. But when we look at the world, we see that this is far from the case. Not only are nations divided, but so are individuals. Many people are hurt and wounded inside, and inner healing is necessary before there can be healing of nations. Others are torn apart by warring elements within, which leave them devastated and depressed. In a war-torn world, torn inside and out, we long for healing and peace.

Pilgrimage as Therapy

We live in an age with a heavy investment in the various forms of therapy. We have set out upon a journey that will lead us to ultimate choices and to the issues of life and death. This is why the uses and abuses of psychology are an important area for our reflection and consideration. Many people seem to have replaced their faith in God with faith in psychological insights. Others, among them committed Christians, shy away from the psychological realm altogether. Still others believe that the findings of the psychologists can help us to understand more fully the adventure of interior exploration. Psychology can certainly help us to see what goes on inside individuals and inside society.

Two great names spring to mind when considering the role of psychology in human development: Sigmund Freud and C. G. Jung. They pioneered the disciplined and systematic exploration of the human soul and uncovered enormous sources of energy that can both heal and destroy. The study of human psychology has proved invaluable in unblocking lines of communication between people and between contrary aspects of our inner selves. It has led us, perhaps, to the threshold where we may encounter the source of new life. By means of psychological techniques, many have been liberated from ignorance about themselves, and placed upon the road leading to wholeness and holiness. Psychology itself, however, stops short, like Moses, of the Promised Land.

Great therapists (especially Jung) understand the limitations of therapy. There is a reverence, a humility, and a reticence that marks the most profound physicians of the human soul. The best of them have helped thousands on the voyage to wholeness. There are many wounded souls in our age who have been restored by contact with what we have called *healing personalities*. The great therapists have this marvelous gift of a healing presence. We know such people in our everyday experience. They are the sort of people it is a sheer pleasure to be with. Their simple presence calms, heals, and restores us. Time spent with such people seems to fly by, even though there might often be some hard work or serious conversation going on. They are the healers, the whole-makers. There are others who seem to bring with them a disrupting presence. Just a few minutes in a room with such a person can leave us limp and exhausted.

We are all engaged in *therapy* one way or another. Our friendships, our families, and our loves are the means by which we are continually renewed, healed, and restored. It is only by contact with others that we grow, that we are transformed. Our commitment to Christ is one that understands him to be the great physician, the healer of all the wounds that afflict men and women. It would be strange indeed if we were not to experience his healing power through the hands of gifted men and women. This is one way Christ has chosen to come to us, to work in us.

We do, however, have a problem with the word *therapy*. It is tied to the medical profession where the relationship of the patient to the doctor tends to be very one-sided. There are wonderful exceptions, but when we go to see our physician it is not usually a meeting between two equals or, more precisely, between two mysteries.

Finding out about things helps. It is not knowing that can be painful. We spend a great deal of our time worrying. "I wonder if the children are all right?" "Did I remember to turn off all the lights?" "I wonder if I have cancer?" Not knowing is a terrible burden and takes up enormous amounts of energy. Yet there are innumerable things we do not know about the world and ourselves, and this *not knowing* makes us vulnerable to those who claim to have some, if not all, of the answers.

All knowledge, especially a supremely saving knowledge (that which heals and nurtures us), comes to us as gift.

Psychology is a gift. Like all gifts, it can be abused. At its best, it is a means by which we move and are moved towards healing and wholeness. It can, on the other hand, help us trivialize terrifying things and enable us to live life only on a superficial level. In fact, it is not unlike *religion,* which can either bring us face to face with the living God or provide us with subtle ways for not facing him. It can expose us. It can hide us. It can open or close us by providing the means by which we can face or avoid confrontation with our innermost selves.

It is in the area of our struggle for perfection that modern psychology has proved most helpful. It has done a great deal to throw light on the path to healing, wholeness, and holiness. This does not mean, of course, that we are wiser or more *spiritual* than our grandparents. We do, however, see things differently. We have a different way of knowing which (we hope) is better suited to our communal and personal survival in this last quarter of the twentieth century. Psychology at its best has opened us up as mysteries. We recognize that the whole of humanity, feelings as well as thoughts, unconscious motives as well as conscious, reflect God's image in us. A human being is a mystery because he is, by definition, the image of God, which is another way of saying the dwelling place of God. Modern psychology has freed many from the fetters of false guilt that smother the image of God in us, and has enabled us to go on pilgrimage again. Others it has thrust out of a too protective nest into the invigorating air of the world outside. We find ourselves in an unfamiliar country like the desert, where new growth in love can take place. Here we find ourselves re-made, re-created in the power of the Holy Spirit.

We cannot, however, embark on the road to wholeness alone. The Christian is not a recluse, but someone who is well aware of the need for fellowship and companionship. The Christian life is the *school of love,* and all the ups and downs of life are part of our education. Both psychology and the Gospel emphasize that we need to love ourselves properly before we can love others. They also teach us that who or what we love makes all the difference to the sort of people we are.

Good or Bad Loves Make Good or Bad Lives

Whom we love makes a difference to who we are. St. Augustine put it this way: "Good or bad loves make good or bad lives." So we have to be careful (as well as truly *carefree*) about our loving.

Our very being cries out for a friend or a lover. When we love someone very much, when we have shared with another the inner secrets, we feel as if we have given our being into their hands. We become vulnerable and open because we realize that we're not complete masters over our lives. The kind of person with whom we fall in love makes all the difference to the shape, quality, and direction of our life. We can think of many occasions when we have been captivated, even infatuated, by a person. When we "fall in love," our whole life is changed. We see everything differently. The person we love colors our vision. We sometimes say that a lover wears rose-colored spectacles. Everything is bathed in a nice pink haze.

If we are deeply affected by our everyday loves, how much more are we affected by our relationship with God? What does it mean to have this intimate relationship with God? How can we express this longing to be nurtured, cherished, caressed by that which is above and beyond us and who, at the same time, moves within each one of us? The deepest longing of the human heart is to be "at home" with God. At least that is the way many of the saints interpreted the deep stirrings within themselves. The psalmist expressed it beautifully when he wrote:

> As the deer longs for the water-brooks,
>   so longs my soul for you, O God.

My soul is athirst for God, athirst for the living God; when shall I come to appear before the presence of God? (Ps. 42:1–2)

Things other than God, which hold our gaze and attention, play the role of *God* in our lives—although most of us would not admit this. Our life, then, is molded and shaped by what concerns us most. Anything that is the subject of our ultimate focus and concern develops godlike qualities, for example, the scientist who is so focused on his research that he has no time for his friends and his family. He cannot *see* them at all. All that matters is the research. It takes up his whole attention, and therefore shapes and molds his life— like a god. These little divinities are present in everyday life. Some of our gods are mortal, with a very short life span. Others manage to dominate us for months and even years. They determine the quality of our life and the shape of our being human. They are the obstacles on the road to wholeness.

It is, therefore, not only other human beings who captivate and infatuate us. Ideas, passions, ambitions, hopes—all sorts of things can take possession of us and rule our lives. When we surrender to an ideal, our whole life is shaped by it, for good or ill. We know people whose life is completely ruled by a conviction. If, for example, you are utterly convinced that everyone is after your money, every moment will be dominated by this obsession. Relationships of trust and love will be closed to you. This is a disease that afflicts some people who are very rich. They can never be sure that anyone really loves them for themselves. They believe that they are loved only for what they have, not for who they are. They have surrendered to the conviction that money dominates human life, and live their lives accordingly. Another block is set up on the road to wholeness.

Healing Requires Surrender

The Christian is invited to surrender his life to the God who was revealed in the life, death, and resurrection of Jesus Christ. The Christian God, therefore, isn't just *any* God. He is particular. His love for us is manifested in a strange and terrible way by the Man-Hanging-on-the-Cross. So if we want to know what human life is really like, we would look (if that were possible) into the mind and heart of our Creator—and the Gospel proclaims that "God was in Christ."

Paying attention to this man Jesus, who is called the

Christ, is what makes and keeps Christian spirituality Christian. It is commitment to him as to a lover that molds and shapes Christians in their being and in their doing. He is the road to wholeness. We can talk about techniques of meditation, ways of prayer, and rules of life, but it is the surrender and commitment to Jesus Christ that makes all the difference between Christian spirituality and other spiritualities. It is Christ who shows us what God is doing by showing us how much God loves us, and Christ who shows us what we are like because he entered totally into our human situation. "I am, all at once, what Christ was, because he was what I am."[1] His life shapes ours. His life forms and transforms us.

This, as we have seen, is not remote from our everyday experience. Our lives are continually being molded and managed by the things that hold our attention and by the people whom we love and admire. We become what we are in our response to our environment. Many human lives are dominated by the acquisitive urge stimulated by advertising, or by the need for power stirred up by intolerance and injustice. It takes a lover or an idea to harness our inner energies for action. The Christian is one who directs his attention in a particular way for the harnessing of all his inner energies for the sake of love. Since we are Christians, Christ is the focus of our loving attention.

Christian commitment demands that we begin with Christ and with no other. Christian experience reveals certain occasions and places where the Christian encounters Christ: in the Bible, in the liturgy, in the preaching, and in the meeting with our fellow human beings, especially with the outcast, the destitute, and the poor.

The Revelation of God in the Hazelnut

Lady Julian of Norwich, the fourteenth-century English mystic, took a tiny hazelnut, placed it in the palm of her hand, and examined it closely. She contemplated it (that is, she really looked at it). In that tiny thing she saw the whole of creation and behind the creation caught a glimpse of the

One who made the hazelnut and also made her. This is what she wrote:

> And he showed me more, a little thing, the size of a hazel-nut, on the palm of my hand, round like a ball. I looked at it thoughtfully and wondered, "What is this?" And the answer came, "It is all that is made." I marvelled that it continued to exist and did not suddenly disintegrate; it was so small. And again my mind supplied the answer, "It exists, both now and for ever, because God loves it." In short, everything owes its existence to the love of God.
>
> In this "little thing" I saw three truths. The first is that God made it; the second is that God loves it; and the third is that God sustains it.[2]

Now take something small in your own hand: a leaf, or a flower. It doesn't matter what it is as long as it's small and natural. Look at it. God made it. God made you. God called you into being. God holds you in being. Look and be still. Such looking is the beginning of prayer. Stillness enables us to pay attention to the loving Other in our midst. Silence pushes us on the path to wholeness.

· 6 ·

What Is Spirituality?

Christianity is the revelation of the summons to full humanity. Part of what it means to be fully human is to rest in God in an attitude of complete trust. We have seen how Lady Julian became deeply aware of her dependence on God by gazing at the hazelnut that rested in the palm of her hand. To be a person is to rest in God's palm in the same simple way as a tiny seed or nut could rest in ours. To realize this one simple thing—our utter reliance on God for all our being and doing—is to have already begun to pray. For what else could our response be to such a mystery but loving and reverent silence?

Life comes to us as a free gift, and we depend absolutely for its maintenance and continuance on the giver. God, the generous sustainer of all life, allows us to mold and shape our lives as we will. The gift of life, however, is so rich and diverse that it requires a spirituality to bind it together in some kind of pattern. It is the arrangement of the various elements and the way that they are held together that make life both challenging and enjoyable.

There are two perspectives from which we can look at the meaning of our life in Christ. The first is theological. We understand ourselves as related to God, the Holy Trinity, in whose image we are made, and who has revealed himself to us in Jesus Christ. The other perspective focuses more on actual human experience, on the unique personal being of each historical human life, rather than on theological statements about our relationship to God. Both perspectives are important.

Julian's vision is a good example of the first perspective. It is objective, like the whole literature of the Bible, and indeed of all literature until the Renaissance. After that, human observation and speculation began to turn inward. Human beings became fascinated with the unique inner world of individual experience. It is this dimension to which we now turn.

How are we to put together the glorious and humbling fact that who we are is a gift utterly dependent on the giver, with the alarming and apparently opposite fact that we have been given the freedom to shape our lives as we will? How can we be both dependent and free at the same time? All we can say at the moment is that, strange as it may seem, human freedom depends on our being able to surrender to the giver of life. We shall be free insofar as we have surrendered our lives to God "whose service is perfect freedom." In fact, human life is meaningless without some act of surrender, and the various spiritualities available to us all invite our submission.

What Is My Purpose? What Is My Meaning?

As we have seen, *spirituality* is one of those umbrella words that covers anything from a serious excursion into Zen Buddhism to a passing interest in astrology. Why are people interested in the unfamiliar spiritual terrain of the East? Human beings are hungry for a sense of purpose and meaning, and when things seem to have dried up at home they are forced to search elsewhere. For many, the well of Western Christianity seems to have dried up. Zen Buddhism has, for example, revived many with its freshness, its humor, and its ability to help people to see life in a new way. It comes like spring rain on a dry and cracked earth. There are other waters, however, which can poison those who drink.

Spirituality is concerned with our yearning for meaning and purpose, and used in its broadest sense can include

many human activities, which, on the surface, do not appear
to be *religious* at all. Consider the excitement of professional
sports—football, baseball, and soccer, for instance—as an
example of a pool of life-giving water in a dry land for the
viewers. How can they have anything to do with spirituality? Watching them on television or "live" absorbs the
passion and interest of a large segment of the population
(mainly male) in an important concentration of energy and
power. Spectator sports slake, for a little while, an inner
thirst. They contribute, for thousands, far more to their sense
of meaning and purpose than any church service. They can
act, however, as a narcotic for many, providing the distrac-
tion that prevents them from asking deeper questions of
meaning.

Some people seem to be content with not asking any
questions at all. They simply live from moment to moment.
Life is certainly not seen as the summons to full humanity,
but rather the summons to what has been called *the marketing
character:* that is, someone who wants to be desirable to as
many people as possible. The human being then sees him- or
herself as a product, as something for sale in the market
place.

Different Spiritualities
Produce Different Personalities

Just as good or bad loves make good or bad lives, so different
ways of looking at the world determine ways people behave
in the world. Life is a free gift, but it can be made to conform
to twisted and contorted patterns. While some make sense of
their lives by refusing to ask deep questions, others make
sense by answering the question of meaning with one
simple answer. Everything gets pushed under to serve the
ruling passion: greed, covetousness, ambition, and even
love.

Consider the great train robbery of 1855. Edward Pierce,
its mastermind or *cracksman*, was a person galvanized rather

than drugged by the passion of his life, a passion that wonderfully concentrated his considerable stock of courage, inventiveness, discipline, strength, skill, and lust upon the single purpose of his life: "I wanted the money."

In short, our spiritual life is our human life directed towards an end or a purpose. It is primarily concerned with knitting together the fragments, experiences, the bits and pieces that go to make up our lives. In a sense, everyone is spiritual, everyone has a spiritual life. It can be, quite simply, a general term for the various ways in which one tries to keep one's life together—or identify someone or something other than oneself that binds the parts of life together.

Spirituality as the pattern in a human being's life that holds him or her (more or less) together is a very ordinary, a very homely thing. It is a far cry from the popular notion of spirituality as an elevated, almost supernatural state of consciousness. There is a stained-glass quality about the word for many people, an unreal quality. The word *spirituality* needs rescuing. It means so much more than pious thoughts. It is concerned with the human hunger for love, meaning, and purpose. It focuses for us the object of our surrender. It deals with the ultimate mystery of human consciousness and with the opposites in our experience: the tension between order and freedom.

I was born. My entrance into the world is one certain and fixed point of reference in an uncertain world. There was no choice. The fact that I exist and that I am myself and no one else was given to me. But saying as much does not really help. Is it possible that I could mean anything? Of course, there are many ways of answering the question of meaning, many of them diabolical and destructive. The point is that everyone has a spirituality—from Mother Teresa of Calcutta to the late Chairman Mao. Our choice of a particular spirituality, a particular way of arranging and gluing together the bits and pieces of our scattered lives, will determine the shape of our character and personality. Everyone struggles towards wholeness. The Christian struggles towards wholeness in Christ.

Christian Spirituality

Christian spirituality is this: human life in its fullness, lived in an ever-deepening and loving surrender to the Spirit of Christ, that Holy Spirit promised, poured out, and always flowing from the heart of the eternal reality that we call *the Father*. It flows for the sake of the redemption and renewal of creation. This Spirit touches us in every part of our lives. We have to bring spirituality down to earth, to our particular circumstances, not in order to keep it there, but to see that it embraces everything to do with the here and now, with our breathing, with our sexuality, with our hopes and aspirations, and with our human fear of death. It is the power of the Spirit that continues to raise us from our deadness. An honest spirituality has to face the central question of our death, because our death is the other certain and fixed point of reference in an uncertain world.

So we find that there are some basic concerns involving all human beings, which we might call *spiritual*. As we have seen, these concerns usually come in the form of questions. Do I matter? Does anyone really love me? What is the meaning of my dying, my particular dying? These are the questions of meaning, of intimacy, and of death that wait in the darkness of every human heart. These are spiritual questions that challenge, stretch, and vex the human spirit.

Christian spirituality, which shapes the Christian character, starts with the affirmation that our summons to personality is set within the context of a marvelous created order that is fundamentally good . . . . "In the beginning God created the heavens and the earth . . . . And God saw that it was good" (Gen. 1:1ff.).

It begins with the revelation of the goodness of creation, and goes on to affirm and proclaim that goodness in all our being and doing. It should avoid like the plague anything that suggests that the world of matter is evil and that the world of the spirit is good. If we look at the world in which we live, we can see that the material can be good and the spiritual evil. The material well-being of the people of the earth is no less a spiritual concern than their inner well-being. The body is not divorced from the spirit, still less is it inferior and evil. To be honest, we have not always been healthy and Christian with regard to our attitude to the body. There has grown up in peoples' minds a picture of the Christian who is a kill-joy, a wet-blanket, a ghost appearing at the feast, as the enemy of honest, full-blooded enjoyment. They suspect that there would be no more "cakes and ale" if Christians had their way!

Christians have often been considered people who are more concerned with externals than with inner dispositions. Some of us get away with professing a Christianity that seems to say that Christ does all our loving for us. We don't have to do anything but keep up appearances. Others of us seem to profess a morality of rules and regulations. Spiritual evils are much harder to spot than visible and material ones. Hatred and malice lurking in the human heart are much harder to detect than mugging, prostitution, or bribery. We naturally go for those things we can easily identify, and miss the deeper, inward, spiritual sins. The outwardly dutiful husband who is faithful in everything except his heart can commit acts of quiet and sophisticated cruelty unreachable by a court of law. The webs of tyranny woven around our personal relationships are many and varied.

Two conclusions, then, come out of this glance at the word *spirituality*. The first is that it is not *necessarily* good. The second is that it is not necessarily otherworldly or escapist. There are spiritualities (and Christianity is one of them) that are deeply involved in political and social realities. If Christian spirituality is concerned with all our being and doing, then it will include the life we share with others as well as our private lives. The New Testament bears witness to this engagement with the world and involvement with one another. "If any one says, 'I love God,' and hates his brother, he is a liar" (1 Jn. 4:20). The mere saying of pious words counts for nothing: "Not every one who says to me, 'Lord, Lord,' shall enter the kingdom of Heaven" (Mt. 7:21).

To sum up, spirituality is another way of talking about our total life, and Christian spirituality is concerned with the Christian life, seen as the totally human life, and as such affirms the value of the body, the material. It denies any dualism between spirit and matter, and refuses, therefore, an escapist view of things. The Christian is not one for whom salvation depends on a release from the body or an escape from the material order. Nor is it narrowly individualistic. We find out who we are only in communion with others. It is above all a person's engagement with inner and outer realities, and it is to the shape of this engagement we must soon turn.

Let us stop for a few moments and think about this summons to full humanity. God is calling us to be persons. What does that mean? How is *personaltiy*, in the Christian sense, expressed? It is expressed in a life shaped and inspired by Christ. Are we ready to ask ourselves some hard questions?

- What are the things that really help me to make sense of my life and that make me feel more of a person?
- What sort of activities have taken on a *religious* significance for me?
- What are the questions I persistently avoid asking?
- Have I answered the questions superficially?
- What sort of person have I become during the past year?
- What do I need to do to respond more fully to Christianity as the revelation of and the summons to full humanity?

Finally, what do our answers to these questions say about the general shape of our lives, our use of time and money, and our commitment to family, friends, and community?

· 7 ·

The Shape of Humanity: The Elements

The Christian personality is shaped (like other personalities) by one ruling passion that binds all the fragments together. That ruling passion is the self-giving love of Christ. This self-giving love, we believe, brings together into the beginnings of harmony all our gifts, powers, and limitations. The Christian person is formed, first and foremost, by being loved and by accepting that love as a free gift. This loving attitude develops the personality in four distinct patterns of relationships. It involves:

- a relatedness to the mystery of being itself, which we call *God*;
- a relatedness to the world that he made, to the created order that he sustains, to our place and stake in the order of things;
- a social relatedness by which we are connected to one another in systems of hierarchy and organization, from the family to the big corporation, from the nation to the world community;
- an inner relatedness that fosters our growth and unfolding as human beings.

It is this final way that is usually identified with spirituality, but the unfolding of the *self* relies on the fostering of the other three relationships and could not develop without them. A healthy spirituality is always concerned with making connections between inner and outer realities, and moves towards the harmonious relationship between God, the world, and our inmost selves.

Spirituality entails confrontation and exposure as well as comfort and security. It proclaims a fearful intimacy, the deep interconnectedness of everything. Let us begin with the world in which we live and our relationship to it.

The Relationship to Things and to the Created Order

Our relationship to the things that God has made requires an attitude of awe and reverence. The more we admire things (which means to look in wonder at them), the less likely we are to hurt or exploit them. So we are called lovingly to admire the things that God has made. The life of prayer is the life of adoration. Another word like adoration is *contemplation*—to look at things with respect and love. When we do that, things have a life and integrity of their own. They are not simply there for us to use and abuse. They are there first to be admired, contemplated, enjoyed simply as they are for what they are. This can be expressed in a simple rule: *we either contemplate or we exploit.* We either admire or we manipulate. We either allow things to be or we twist and use them for our own purposes.

This basic enjoyment of things means sensing our oneness with creation, of seeing ourselves rooted in the earth, of feeling the sea in our veins and appreciating our solidarity with the stars. We are like the earth, the sea, and the stars. We are creatures, and as creatures we are one with the whole created order. This basic sense of oneness is something that many of us have lost. It is something so simple and straightforward, and yet it has become remote and strange to many of us.

The poet Anne Sexton expresses this admiration, this oneness, beautifully:

Teresa of Ávila said:
I have no defense against affection.
I could be bribed with a sardine.
O dear Teresa,
I could be bribed likewise.
The hand in mine,
or the chapel inside a bean.

. . .

Ávilan of Teresa
who taught her nuns
to dance for joy
in the cloister,
a dance of joy,
unto God,
as the birds fling
themselves into the air
as the human face moves
knowing it will be kissed.[1]

The whole of the created order is full of the presence of God: "The chapel inside a bean." It is in the ordinary everyday things like beans and sardines that we can *admire* God.

As we have seen, many spiritualities tend to undervalue the material, the flesh, and the world of time and space. They fail to take this life, the here and now, very seriously. Christianity, because it is unashamedly materialistic, is concerned with the local, with the particular. God's quiet presence is to be discerned in sardines, garden vegetables, and upturned faces. He is in the ordinary and in the commonplace, and the discipline of prayer is to help us cultivate a patient watchfulness so that we can see the Creator being himself.

It is early on a winter morning, the birds (three jays, a cardinal, and several unidentified finches) flutter and settle on the birdfeeder hanging on a tree outside the study window. There is a blanket of snow, and the sun is a harsh red disc appearing over the hill. The world is coming to life.

The creative Presence pervades all things. His electrifying power is everywhere. The picture is idyllic, but nevertheless true. There are other realities in this world, grim and terrible, which we will have to face, but for the moment we are thinking of God as Creator. When we come to the suffering side of life in this world, we shall have to enter the strange mystery of God as the Redeemer who enters that suffering in us and for us. That is why our relationship to things is not sufficient. We need other relationships: to others, to ourselves, to God. Although these other relationships are sometimes painful, they bring us to the fullness of life.

God is Creator, Savior, Spirit. He is the One who made us and continues to recreate us through the energizing power of the Holy Spirit. Our human life is centered in praise and adoration. It is loving admiration. Prayer is the offering of creation back to the Father through the Holy Spirit. This is not a remote philosophical doctrine about the being of God, but the basic principle of human life. We breathe back to God the breath (spirit) he breathed into us at our beginning. It is an act of love. Its expression is beyond words. "Nothing," wrote a ninth-century theologian

> can be said worthily about God. Hardly a single noun or verb, or any part of speech can be used appropriately of God in the strict sense. . . . And yet, ever since the Fall, poverty-stricken human reason has been laboring with these words, these visible signs, to suggest and to give some sort of a hint of the sublime richness of the Creator.[2]

Our words about God are hopelessly inadequate, but they are all we have. We must not forget that they cannot and do not tell the whole truth. They do not plumb the depths of or exhaust the mystery. They do not, in any sense, allow us to understand or control God with our ideas. We can discern only "the outskirts" of his ways.

Open and receptive silence is the appropriate response to God as Creator. The silence can sometimes be disturbing, for it reminds us that we are creatures. We are not gods. We are destined to die. The silent waiting on God is the beginning of our learning to rejoice in and not be terrified by our creatureliness. The emphasis on our creatureliness is very important. It will prevent our spiritual exercises from degenerating into easy rules for enlightenment. The fact that we are creatures helps us simply to *admire* God in the things he has made rather than organize a program of self-improvement.

The Relationship to Others

Our view of the world is often related (if sometimes only remotely) to the stories we heard as children, to the picture of things we formed in school and received through the media. Our society is bound together by a common memory (which we stir up on July 4th and on Thanksgiving Day) and by a common hope. We describe ourselves, in hope, as "one nation under God." Our motto is *e pluribus unum*—out of many people, one nation. What it means to be an *American* human being relies on an undergirding of myths, sagas, and stories that all Americans more or less share: ideas of freedom, or self-determination, of the classless society in which everyone who was willing to work could share in the abundant life. These ideas are part of our history. They bind people together. It is often an inspired leader of great vision who can bring a fragmented and confused people together. We sometimes find unity not by surrendering to a passion but by surrendering to a person. We call such a person a charismatic leader, a person who has the gift of creating a committed community around his vision, who can believe in it, celebrate it, and proclaim it. Not all charismatic leaders, however, are filled with the charisma of the Holy Spirit. Adolf Hitler was a charismatic leader. He was able to create and inspire a community of dedicated men and women willing to celebrate and live out his vision in the world. The vision, alas, was evil, and the consequences of that celebration tragic beyond measure. If we have no vision of our own, we are destined to be part of someone else's dreaming.

We long for relatedness. Inevitably the question arises, "How am I related to all those other human beings?"

Political, social, and economic considerations come crowding in, probing our relationships not only to our friends and neighbors but also to our fellow human beings in the most remote corners of the earth.

The Relationship to Ourselves

When we begin to see the way all things are united in God, we realize that everything there is is utterly dependent on him. The world, other people, even ourselves come to us as free gifts. In our relationship to God in prayer, we experience the mystery of God continually giving us back to ourselves. There is that strange expression we often use: "I don't feel quite myself this morning," or "I don't know what came over him. He certainly wasn't his usual self." That self that we guard so jealously is often mislaid. God is always calling us back to our true selves, giving us back what was lost. Sometimes life becomes so complicated or we are so overburdened by something we've done or somebody we've hurt that it seems impossible that we should ever find our true selves again.

In Christ we are continually found and brought to the place where we are "at home," where we can truly be ourselves. Even who we are is a gift because we have no existence through our own efforts or even by right. "All is gift," wrote Fenelon (1651–1715), the archbishop of Cambrai, in France. "He who receives the Gift is himself the first gift he receives." St. Augustine, writing of all things coming as a gift from God, affirms the same thing: "They were all gifts from God. . . . His gifts are good and the sum of them all is my own self." To grasp that (or at least to catch a glimpse of that) is to have already entered the divine mystery in the face of which prayer needs neither justification nor explanation. It is to understand that we do not make ourselves so much as receive ourselves as gift. That is the point of our waiting in the stillness. We wait, and we receive, and what we receive in the power of the Holy Spirit is the indwelling Presence that restores us and gives us back to ourselves.

Our life in God also opens us to transcendence. That is to

say, the life of prayer is always opening up new areas in our hearts we scarcely knew existed. There is always more. In fact, there are vast areas of the human soul that have yet to be uncovered. A totally human being understood from a Christian perspective is one who is open to going beyond what he knows of himself. No one can ever fully understand himself because he is finally related to the incomprehensible God. The most real thing about us is that relationship—not our hang-ups, our neuroses, or our habits; and it certainly is not our sin. The most real thing about us is God calling us to himself.

> Blessed be the God and Father of our Lord Jesus Christ, who hath blessed us with all spiritual blessings in heavenly places in Christ: according as he hath chosen us in him before the foundation of the world, that we should be holy and without blame before him in love: having predestined us unto the adoption of children by Jesus Christ to himself, according to the good pleasure of his will, to the praise of the glory of his grace, wherein he hath made us accepted in the beloved (Eph. 1:3–6, KJV).

The Relationship to God

We now come to the relationship that logically should come first. The crown of everything is our relationship to God. It is this primary covenant that undergirds all the others. We must remember, however, that this relationship is not separate or exclusive, but is expressed in all our other relationships, particularly in the ones we have with our fellow human beings.

Our fundamental relationship with God and with one another is a mystery. Indeed, it is the relationship between two mysteries: God and ourselves. The human heart is God's hiding place. It is a place of waiting. This is a far cry from much conventional religion, from manipulative pieties, from techniques for enlightenment that want to organize and program inner development. Christian spirituality affirms that a human being's fundamental attitude is one of waiting and of adoration before the mystery of Being, Being that he senses not only stirring within the universe, but also within his fellow human beings—and within himself. When that sense of the stirring of the Spirit is absent, we are confronted with a devastating feeling of loneliness and desolation. We are like orphans in a foreign country. We are lost and afraid. The loneliness can be transformed into solitude if we wait: Just as the vast emptiness of the human heart can become the place of encounter with the Holy Spirit. This desert, this wilderness within, is precisely the theater for that encounter that we dread, and for which we yearn. We dread it because we know that to encounter God is to change and sometimes to change dramatically. We yearn for it, because we know that it is only through this encounter with God that we truly come alive.

Pause now, and ask yourself four questions concerning your spiritual life or the spiritual life of your community or parish.

- How do I foster and nurture my relationship to God?
- Do I have a genuine reverence and admiration for the creation?
- How am I related to others; to my immediate circle, to my local community, to the human family?
- Am I growing and developing at all inside? Am I open to the inner workings of the Holy Spirit?

· 8 ·

The Shape of Humanity:
The Harmony

We have described the Christian life as a journey, as progress through the desert towards a promised goal, and as the gradual and deliberate harmonization of our lives within a fourfold pattern of meaning. This pattern of relationships to the world, to others, to ourselves, and to God can be compared to the playing of a symphony by a great orchestra. We are all players related to one another, but we don't all play the same tune. Some carry the melody for a while, while others stick to the ongoing bass rhythms that keep the music moving. At some moments we don't play at all, but wait until it is our turn once again.

We do not develop all four relationships at once. At times, some of us have to have a special concern, for example, with the world and its problems—with social and political concerns. Others have to concentrate on relationships nearer home. At some point in our lives we have to take stock of ourselves, of who and where we are in life. We are all at various times called to the quiet and open contemplation of God. It is all of us all together that make the music, and the symphony requires each one of us playing the part that has been given at a particular moment with all our heart. The trouble is that so many of us assume that we should all be playing exactly the same thing at the same time. Not so. The

61

person passionately concerned for the environment, the parent struggling to bring up a family, the man discovering more of himself through psychoanalysis, and the woman called to a life of contemplative prayer are all part of one great symphony and, truly, are not in rival groups. Insofar as each one of us is committed to Christ, each of us is in harmony with the others, no matter how strange the tune may sound.

This is an ideal picture. There are, sometimes, awful sounds, terrible dissonances, but it is as well to remember that we are called to enjoy a harmony, a pattern of relationship given to us by Christ. Each one of us needs to learn to listen more intently to the tunes others are playing and to the deeper rhythms that bind us all together.

The pattern of relationship is expressed supremely in the Bible in the covenant as the source of our relatedness to God and to each other; in the liturgy as the drama of this relationship; in the ongoing life of the church (the tradition) as the guardian of all our relationships; and in the individual human heart as the celebrant of the peculiar and specific relationships that make the Christian life Christian. Through them, the Spirit acts continually to purify the vision, call the community to a change of heart (repentance), and stir it up for service in the world. There is no Christian life without a community fed by the word of God as contained in the Scriptures, and sustained and nurtured by the sacramental life. There are no Christians who "go it alone." There is no private spirituality. Christian spirituality is essentially a sharing in a common life, nourished by a common vision.

Interchange and Balance

Some people overemphasize their relationship to the world and to others at the expense of their relationship to God and to their inner selves. When this happens, worldly and social concerns may become shallow, empty, and baseless, and soon lose their vitality. When the relationships to God and our innermost selves are overemphasized, they can be easily cut off from their moorings on firm ground and become selfish and self-absorbing. There are some within the Body of Christ, called to emphasize a particular aspect of the whole. The monk or the nun may be called upon to emphasize, in the church and for the sake of the church, our primary relationship to God. Others will be called to focus their concern on environmental, political, or social issues. Still others will be called upon to concentrate on the healing of inner wounds so that free relationships can take place.

So you see we need one another in the Christian family. If you are of a mystical turn of mind, you may well need those fellow Christians who will make you look at the world and its needs, its hopes, and aspirations. There are other people, however, who will need to hear what you have to say concerning the relationship God has with all human beings. This will help them focus their social and political concerns. Alone, each one's vision is partial and defective. Together, we can catch a glimpse of the glory, of the wholeness, the healing, and the holiness promised to all. This is not only a vision of what might be: it is also a vision of what actually is.

A good way to examine our spiritual life for balance is to ask ourselves those four basic questions that we posed at the end of the last chapter. Let us rephrase them and look at them again.

- How do I relate (how am I related) to the created order? Do I exploit or reverence the environment?
- How do I relate (how am I related) to other people? Do I understand that there is a basic unity among all the children of God?
- How do I relate (how am I related) to myself? Do I escape into myself, or do I carve out *a desert place within* to be the dwelling place of God? How do I deal (indeed, can I deal) with the darkness in myself?
- How do I relate (how am I related) to God? Is he just the God of my own imaginings, or is he the God of the Exodus who continually does the unexpected?

This set of questions, answered honestly, can also help a parish test its communal spiritual life. Parishes, like people, often emphasize two of the relationships at the expense of the other two. Spirituality is often opposed to social concern because it is identified with only two of the relationships (to ourselves and to God). The socially active parish, on the other hand, frequently neglects these last two, and concentrates on the world and others. A balanced spirituality requires us to participate as fully as possible in all four.

We need to be reminded of our first principle: *All is gift, and the gift that God gives us is himself.* All our striving and all our efforts are to be seen in the light of this fact. The Christian adventure is the means by which we become more open, more receptive to God's gift of himself to us in Jesus. "For God so loved the world that he gave his only Son, that whoever believes in him should not perish but have eternal life" (Jn. 3:16). The Christian is the one who is born again into that wider reality. As we have seen, this is not to say that all have to have a special stunning experience as Paul did on the road to Damascus. This is given to some but not to all. Our second birth may take years. Whichever way it comes, it will mean risking everything. The human adventure brings with it the possibility of shipwreck. There is a sense in which shipwreck, total failure, is a necessary experience for the fullness and maturity of the Christian. This is not, of course, to say that we are to deliberately head our little ship for the rocks in a wild act of self-destruction. It does mean, however, that the Christian, in following Christ, must expect to encounter suffering. Christianity is the religion of those willing to lose everything for the sake of love.

There is no way through without risk. There is no safe way for the Christian who follows the way of the Cross. There are, however, guides and signposts placed along our path by the accumulated experience of centuries. We can have some idea of the landscape, some notion of the powers and influences we're likely to meet. Above all, we can travel in hope because the Christian marches not in his own strength, but in the power of the Spirit. By it the very things that seem destructive and menacing can be transformed into agents of growth in love. In the end, nothing "will be able to separate us from the love of God in Christ Jesus our Lord" (Rom. 8:39). It is this conviction, and this alone, that has enabled countless men and women to hazard an adventure far beyond their imaginings and sense of competence. Theirs is a strength that comes not from arrogance but from humility.

The virtue of humility is the virtue of seeing things clearly *as they are*. We have already faced the dangers of being inflated by our experiences. We know that we neither own our experiences nor have we caused them. We inherit the Kingdom and enter into it as a gift and as a privilege. We do not plan it, construct it, or earn it. Our experience of God is given to us as members of a community, and as those who have *emptied* themselves and wait to receive the gift.

To Leave All and Follow Christ

Without the creative and apparently "mad" people who take the Gospel literally, and stir up the hearts and minds of their contemporaries, the world would be a poorer place. There have always been Christians, in every generation, who, in a special way, remind us of the radical call to follow Christ.

There is a story of an old man who, after his retirement, devoted himself unreservedly to work in his parish. He was known for his loving concern for others and his dedication to the life of prayer. In fact, he had the marks of sainthood. His wife, unfortunately, had no sympathy for him and regarded his devotion to God as morbid. One day at the Eucharist, he heard the uncompromising words of the Gospel: "Go and sell all that thou hast and give to the poor, and thou shalt have treasure in heaven, and come and follow me." The words came like a thunderbolt. He emptied his pockets of what money he had into the poor box at the church door and started to walk. He headed for a well-known place of pilgrimage over 100 miles away.

When he failed to come home for either breakfast or lunch, his wife notified the police. He was found about thirty miles from home, walking through a small village. The local doctor saw that he was admitted to a mental hospital. The man made no protest, told his story calmly and simply, and accepted without complaining what had happened to him. The psychiatrist was very sympathetic, gave the man no treatment, but did insist that he eat a good breakfast. His wife, reluctantly, agreed to his discharge and took him home.

Some 1,600 years earlier, another man in a church in Alexandria heard the very same words during the Eucharist. They hit him so hard that he immediately left for the desert and lived a life of heroic discipline until his death. Many people followed him. His name was Anthony. His followers formed themselves into communities and drew up a rule of life. This was the beginning of Christian monasticism. As we know, St. Anthony was canonized. The other man was nearly certified. It is not always easy to tell the difference between the creative madness of a St. Anthony and the destructive patterns of self-absorption.

Let us take another pause, and take a long look at our personal commitment to Jesus Christ. How has it changed over the years? Where is it half-hearted and afraid? Has our commitment grown cold? How do we keep in touch with Christ? Do we foster a life that stretches out to others and to the world for which Christ died? Do we meet Christ in those two special places (the Bible and the Eucharist)?

· 9 ·

Prayer and Experience: Solitude and Community

The self is God-given, the most precious of all created gifts, but it can become a trap to enslave us. We can be led astray very easily by the nagging demands of the self, and it is hard sometimes to maintain a balance between self-neglect and downright selfishness.

The relationship we have to our innermost selves is its most dangerous when it comes to the life of prayer. It can lead us into a dream world that has little or nothing to do with the world around us. It can provide a nice escape into the self under the guise of prayer.

The developing person needs continually to test for reality by relating the inner world of the self to the outer world of everyday life. It is important to have friends who will point out our failures to make the connection between these inner and outer realities.

Talking and Listening—to Whom?

Another problem in our relationship to ourselves is that it is not always easy to tell sometimes whether we are talking and listening to God when we pray or whether we are merely talking and listening to ourselves. That is why we have to develop a fourfold pattern of relationships, not only to ourselves, but to the world around us, to other people, and to God. Without these other relationships, we get bogged down in long monologues and imagine that we are praying. When we are aware of them, prayer can truly develop into a dialogue that enriches and refreshes the spirit. Without these other relationships that keep us down-to-earth, we can find ourselves developing personal habits of prayer that are essentially transactional in nature. That is to say, we fall into the trap of bargaining with God and complaining when things don't turn out (as we think) for the best.

The Experience of God and the God of Experience

There is the story of St. Philip Neri (1515–1595) who used his sense of humor to point out the unreliability and ambiguity of experience. One day one of his followers came to tell him about a delightful vision of the Blessed Virgin Mary, which had elated and warmed him. St. Philip told him that the next time she appeared to him, he was to spit in her eye. When he did so, the devil's face was at once revealed!

It is not difficult to see the point of this story. An experience or vision of reality can be the means by which we imagine that we have trapped that reality. It is as if we own the experience, or worse, as if we made the experience. As we shall see later, an intense experience tends to blow us up with a sense of our own importance; and instead of it being my *experience*, it becomes *my* experience.

The principle is this: we can know God, but in a veiled and hidden way. His love is an invitation into mystery. "No one can see God and live." Personal experience can lead us to imagine that we somehow have a handle on God. It can lead to the deadliest of spiritual diseases: the inability to distinguish our own will from God's.

So the developing relationship we have to our innermost selves is a very deceptive and subtle one. It should not, however, lead us to imagine that we are in a hopeless position with regard to the life of genuine prayer. We have the world in which we live; we have our family, our friends, and the fellowship of the church to help test the reality of our spiritual lives.

Think, for a moment, of those relationships that have, from time to time, saved you from getting trapped inside yourself. Sometimes it only takes a strong word from someone who cares about us to shatter the little illusions we have built for ourselves. At other times, the shattering but healing word comes through the turn of events. Suddenly something happens that makes us realize what we've been up to. It is then that we begin to understand the marvelous healing power of a forgiving and reconciling friendship or the grace that flows from being part of an open and loving community.

Exodus: Journey into God

As we have seen, the spiritual life is like the movement from Egypt through the desert into the Promised Land. It is an Exodus experience. It is a journey in God, to God, and with God. The life of prayer is a desert pilgrimage, full of promise and excitement. We will have to endure the dying of our neatly ordered interpretation of the Gospel, because a free relationship, a liberating covenant with God, requires an openness to infinite possibilities. We are the ones born of the Spirit. "The wind blows where it wills, and you hear the sound of it, but you do not know whence it comes or whither it goes; so it is with everyone who is born of the spirit" (Jn. 3:8).

We are not, however, left without guidance in our spiritual lives. We know who we are (children of the God who revealed himself to us in Jesus Christ), and we know where we are going (to the One who made us and who loves us). The theater of our being and of our doing is not withdrawn space or guarded moment cut out of a busy life. It is in the everyday business of living that the wounding and healing of human beings takes place. But the everyday business of living requires moments of solitude and silence, just as our fundamental relationships to the world, to others, and to ourselves need the explicit and special affirmation of our basic relationship to God. It is in silence and solitude that this special relationship is expressed. If we don't take time out to be still, to be quiet, to wait, the other relationships soon deteriorate.

Experience of Solitude

The experience of solitude is necessary because only in solitude and silence does the living God reveal himself in this special way as the binding source of all that is. The veil is lifted, and we begin to see the wonderful possibilities of life together that surround and inhabit us. This means that, at our worst and darkest moments, we can affirm that we are God's handiwork, that his image has marked us forever, that the most real thing about us is the Holy Spirit who dwells in every human heart. He is that loving otherness in the depths of the newborn baby. We may be fundamentally and utterly nothing, we may be creatures marked for death, but we are peculiar beings whose very emptiness has been designed to be inhabited by nothing less than the living God. And it is in the living God that we meet one another

The life of prayer revolves around two poles: solitude and community. God is encountered in both places.

Society and Solitude:
Twin Poles of Living in the Spirit

Who am I? We have seen that the Biblical images describing the creation of humankind help us to think about what and who we are: dust yet spirit, mortal yet alive with the life of the word of God, alone yet made members of a new creation by his outpoured Spirit. This is what we affirm: I am a new woman or man in Christ. "In it [the water of Baptism] we are buried with Christ in his death. By it we share in his resurrection. Through it we are reborn by the Holy Spirit" (*The Book of Common Prayer*, p. 306).

These are theological statements, solemn and edifying. The images are powerful, and so are the concrete actions that they accompany in the baptismal service. Together they help to initiate us, to take us over the threshold into life in a different dimension.

When we are born into our natural family, we begin life as social beings related to others, dependent upon them and responsive to them. At the same time, we begin our personal existence as unique individuals, and we commonly lose no time in claiming this uniqueness. Indeed, we are encouraged to feel special, to emphasize our differences. Everything within reach is explored and is seen, somehow, as extensions of ourselves—noses, eyeglasses, and the dog's ear. People, too, are seen as being there just for our benefit. The growing baby cannot, at first, distinguish between himself and his world. It is all one. People and the things around him are his. As we grow older we begin to see the difference between ourselves and the things around us. We find that we need both solitude and company if we are to grow as persons. Indeed, all of our life is lived in tension between the two poles of society and solitude.

Mary: A Model for Christians

We have two marvelous pictures in our Christian heritage that help us to understand these two poles. God comes to us in solitude and stillness. He also comes to us in society and community. Mary, the mother of Jesus, is a model for us of the role of solitude. She is also the model of Christian society. She is an image of the church.

First, let us take a look at Mary as an image of Christian solitude. She waited in the stillness and became the mother of the Christ, the *bearer* of God, and is a sign that every human being is to be just that—a God-bearer in the world. She is a glorious sign that every human being is a container of the uncontainable.

What happened to Mary physically must happen to us spiritually. We, like her, are invited to become the dwelling place of God. We, like her, are to wait for the overshadowing of the Spirit so that Christ can be born in us, so that Bethlehem can happen now in the heart of the believer. Such birth-giving comes only in solitude. "And Mary said, 'Behold I am the handmaid of the Lord; let it be unto me according to your word," (Lk. 1:38).

So Mary is the model for Christian men and women of the waiting in solitude for the creative power of God to come to us so that we can *give birth* to outgoing love for the sake of the world.

This may sound somewhat fanciful, but it is not that remote from actual everyday human experience, especially the experience of creative people. Whenever we prepare to do anything creative: write a letter, bake a cake, let alone paint a picture or write a story, there is a period of gestation. We're pregnant with a thought, an idea, a project, and it so builds up inside us that, in the end, we have to *give birth*. Unfortunately, human beings can become pregnant with monstrous as well as with beautiful things. Hatred, vice, and cruelty can grow in the human heart and sometimes burst destructively on the people all around.

The Christian is the one who, like Mary, is pregnant with Christ. The mystics saw every human being as a Bethlehem where Christ was born anew for the saving of the world.

Think, for a moment, of your various *pregnancies*. Perhaps some of them were very short, giving birth to something minor and relatively unimportant. Other *pregnancies* can take a long time to come to term. Years go by, and then it happens. You do something that you've been thinking about for ages. We may even regret that we have given birth to pettiness, unkindness, and insensitivity. The important thing to remember is that the chief energy at work is always the Holy Spirit bringing Christ to birth in us so that we may be what we are meant to be, like Mary, the dwelling place of God.

Those who *give birth* to Christ in their hearts, or better, allow Christ to be born in them, are called Christians. Mary is not only an image for the individual Christian, she is also a model for the community of Christians.

We are using *model* here in the sociological sense. It means not a pattern of perfection we are to strive to imitate, but a new perspective, a new way of looking at something. Mary is a model of the church; first, in her personal life, she provided God with a place where the Incarnation could take place. Salvation began in her. Jesus took flesh in her womb. So the church, the Body of Christ, comes to be among us. Through the working of the Holy Spirit, the church is made visible and audible in the Christian community for the world.

In the Christian story, God works through the free cooperation of men and women, made in his image, and endowed with mysterious grace of liberty.

The second side of the sign of the Virgin Mary is her lowliness. She was chosen by God as Israel was, for no distinction or powers of her own. She was an obscure Jewish woman, a nonentity in her village. The *Magnificat* celebrates her exaltation and the fulfillment in her of God's promise to Abraham. God acted personally through Mary's freedom, through invitation and response, and so he acts in us as members of the church. It is a slow, patient, almost imperceptible action most of the time—although he can blaze out like a meteor when he wills to do so and finds in us a corresponding will to meet him—to bring the Kingdom into our midst.

Mary stands as a sign at the beginning of the Incarnation. So she stands also at the Cross, with her Son, in the anguish and fidelity of her human love. The *Pietà* is also an image of the church. The woman holds Christ in her arms for the world, in an act of love and faith, unfathomable in the depth of its suffering and its generosity.

Christ is present in the church in the arena of human choice and experience and by the working of his Spirit. He does not overrule our liberty of choice, but waits upon it to make himself known in healing and welcoming love to all. This presence and this working occurs in us, his church, and involves us in the suffering of the Cross.

To be a Christian, then, is to be part of a believing community. We need to be able to enjoy solitude so that, when we are with others, we can truly enjoy them without having to control, possess, or manipulate them. We also need the fellowship of the believing community to help us interpret all our different experiences.

Part Two

——

CHRIST THE CENTER, REVEALER OF THE FATHER IN THE SPIRIT

——

· 10 ·

Prayer:
Becoming Human in Christ

We come now to the heart of Christian spirituality. As we
have seen, what makes Christian spirituality *Christian* is
Christ. The Christian does not merely seek special experiences that foster the development of a certain *condition of
soul* when he prays. He is engaged in a relationship with
God whom he encounters as a personal reality. Christ is the
focus and seal of that relationship. He ratifies it, as it were. In
Christ was revealed what Baron von Hügel described as:

> the altogether unsuspected depth and inexhaustibleness of
> human Personality, and of this Personality's source and ana-
> logue in God, of the simplicity yet difficulty and never ending-
> ness of the access of man to God and of the ever-preceding
> condescension of God to man.[1]

In other words, Christians believe that in Christ we are
accessible to God and to one another. This is what it means to
be human: one who is open to God and to others. To be
human, then, is to be rooted in Christ in such a way that all
our being and doing flows from him. St. Paul puts it this
way:

> Be rooted in him;
> Be built in him;

> Be consolidated in the faith you were taught;
> . . .in him you have been brought to completion.
> . . .you were buried with him,
> you were raised to life with him (Col. 2:7, 10, 12, NEB).

The tradition of Christian worship also shows us how to be human in Christ. Let us now look at the various ways we can look at the Christ in whom Christian prayer is rooted.

> And the Word was made flesh [*here the old priest lowers himself on one knee*] and dwelt among us, (and we beheld his glory, the glory as of the only begotten of the Father,) [*here the priest begins to hoist himself up again*] full of grace and truth. [*The people mumble their response,* "Thanks be to God"] (Jn. 1:14, KJV).

Some of us (particularly those of us who are older and who were brought up in the Anglo-Catholic tradition) remember how the Eucharist used to end with these words. This was in "the good old days" before liturgical reform swept away certain additions from before and after the central portion of the Eucharist. The *last Gospel,* as it was called (Jn. 1:1–14), had come to take the place of the deacon's cry, "Go, it is ended," which concluded the old Roman Catholic mass. This cry has been restored in the new Prayer Book: "Go in peace, to love and serve the Lord." This dismissal sends us out into the world to share what we have received at the Lord's Table.

Now that our new Prayer Book incorporates more of the ancient form of the Eucharist, perhaps we can reflect with profit upon the reasons why that first chapter of John was, at one time, seen as a fitting epilogue to the whole service.

We have seen that Christian spirituality has to do with the way Christians make sense of their life, by ordering it under one supreme love, the love of Christ. We have also seen that Christ, the Word of God, reveals to us the meaning of being human. The way that we make sense of our lives is not by imposing something upon it, but by receiving and making our own the gift of new life in Christ. Hence, it is important for us to focus on what the Bible and what Christians throughout the ages have meant when they called Jesus *the*

Christ. Exploration of the meaning and significance of Christ is called *Christology.*

Christology is a vast subject, full of complexities and subtleties, and one which has exercised the best minds in the church throughout the centuries. Christians have produced hymns, liturgies, sermons, and treatises on every aspect of Christology. They have also produced heresies: wrong-headed versions of the Christian experience. Here we can consider only a tiny fragment of this immense inheritance, as it illuminates the Christian life of prayer. How we understand Christ will make all the difference to our praying, since he is the one to whom and in whom we pray. If we see Christ as a revolutionary leader, our prayer life will be very different from that of someone who sees him as an intensely personal savior. There have been and are some Christians, however, who see him as both of these at once.

What is your picture of Christ? What sort of person is he? What does he look like? Think of all the many ways in which Christ has been portrayed in art and in drama. What is your favorite picture or crucifix? Your answer will throw light on your prayer life. In fact, it will throw light on the whole of your life. See if you can find a book with lots of images of Christ (like Roland Bainton's *Behold the Christ*[2]). Take time to look at each picture carefully. What does each one say about Christ? Or look at the crucifix. Some ancient ones have Christ crowned as a king, reigning from the Cross. Those made in the Middle Ages have Christ's body twisted and torn in pain to emphasize human suffering. Some modern crucifixes combine the two images of the reigning Christ and the suffering Jesus in one figure. Each one tells a story. Each one illuminates a little of the mystery. Which image speaks most deeply to you?

Ways of Looking at Christ

Doctrines about Christ, who he was and what he did, sprang up out of particular situations. Some people would say: "Christ wasn't fully human. Christ was more divine." The community of the Church would react, and say, "Well, that doesn't square with our experience of Christ. We believe he was indeed fully human." The formulation of dogma by the church seems to have been stimulated by the appearances of mistaken teaching or incomplete statements of doctrine. These were called heresies.

The church is the Body of Christ, and we can see that her growth follows laws like those of biological development. There is, for instance, a law called *anaphylaxis,* which keeps an organism true to form. If one could, for example, inject the essence of cat into a dog, the dog would not become something like a cat. The law of anaphylaxis would protect it by preserving its *dogness.* It would either remain unchanged or die of shock. The church's reaction to mistaken teaching has been compared to anaphylaxis. The church can tolerate a certain amount of mistaken doctrine, but when the dose becomes too heavy, a reaction sets in, and the heresy is rejected.

Consider the history of Christian thought about Christ and the ways in which Christians have prayed to him and in him, in the light of this biological analogy. It was in answer to inaccurate or one-sided statements about Christ that councils and theologians spelled out their definitions of Christ and the Christian experience from earliest times until our own day. Sometimes a way of praying developed first, and the teaching about Christ came afterwards. When, for example, people who had been brought up on Greek ideas prayed, they tended to look down on the body and to see the spiritual life as otherworldly. We should not be surprised, therefore, to discover that their view of Christ tended to emphasize his divinity at the expense of his humanity.

Christology is an effort to explain how Jesus can be a historical figure from a specific time and place and at the same time be the divine Son of God; how the eternal Word could take flesh; how a woman could bear God.

Two Ways of Looking at Christ: Two Ways of Praying

There were two early ways of looking at Christ, one we have just mentioned, coming from Greek circles, and the other coming from Jewish circles. The Greek way of looking at Christ was called *docetic* (from the Greek verb "to seem"). A docetic Christology is one that says Christ only *seemed* to be human. His coming in the flesh was only an appearance. God is pure spirit and could not express himself within the life of the flesh and the world. Many early sects adopted some form of a docetic Christ, and this not-quite-human Christ reappears from time to time in the various ways Christians say their prayers. The Christ to whom we pray is often very remote. He certainly isn't someone who could get himself really mixed up in human affairs, nor someone to whom we could bring our dingiest and most shocking needs and problems.

Those who believed the other way of looking at Christ (coming from Jewish circles) took the opposite position. Jesus was a man upon whom special dignity was conferred by God. Those who believe Christ to be a sort of *adopted* son of God, as well as those seeing Christ as moral hero or the greatest of human teachers, are in this line of thought. When we pray to this Christ, we are praying to one who is very close to us. He is our brother.

The central difficulty for our understanding of Christ is how to hold together in one mind and one formula these two statements: Jesus Christ is God and Jesus Christ is man. Both are true. Both affect the life of prayer. Since they are statements about two great mysteries (God and man), only a metaphor or picture can bring them together. Efforts to explain the mystery by trying to fit them together like bits of a puzzle simply do not work. The gap between the two statements is not just a break in logic or a plank missing from a bridge. It is the heart of the mystery to which adoration is the only adequate response.

Still, we cannot do without words. Christians have always tried to put their deep experience of God into the clearest possible language.

Modern thinkers present us with new ways of looking at Christ, some of them old ways in disguise. Some see Jesus Christ as the great liberator, as the one who frees human beings from social and political tyrannies. Others see him as a sign of the fully developed person. Still others find meaning for their own lives by reflecting on the story of Jesus. He is at once the cosmic Christ and the *man for others*. He is *Jesus Christ, Superstar*. He is the Jesus of *Godspell*. We struggle, just as the early Christians did, to put into words what Jesus Christ means to us in a way that our contemporaries can understand. We try to use language that will express, in a modern way, the deep truth of Jesus Christ's ultimate significance.

These efforts help us to approach the mystery of God-in-flesh, to understand more and more about it, but they never quite satisfy us. Words never do. Like all human words about God, they are signposts pointing towards a divine reality, but they remain at a distance from that reality.

The Anglican poet W. H. Auden wrote:

Dogmatic theological statements are to be comprehended neither as logical propositions nor as poetical utterances; they are to be taken rather as shaggy dog stories; they have a point, but he who tries hard to get it will miss it.

The life of prayer is very important here because it enables us to make the important distinction between the Christ we grasp and the Christ who grasps us. The Christ we grasp is always changing. When we were teenagers, Christ was, quite likely, a superversion of ourselves, although more ascetic and probably something of a prig. As we grew up, so did the Christ we grasped. The Christ who grasps each of us, although hidden from us, is "the same today, yesterday, and forever." This Christ held you when you were seventeen in spite of your attempts to make him in your own image.

In some ways, theological definitions are better at denying than affirming. They can say better what Jesus Christ is not. He is not simply a good man. He is not simply a divine being pretending to be man. He is not half-man and half-God. The Scriptures and our Christian heritage present him to us with the claim that he is "one with the Father," that this man is indeed God, and that our response to him in faith is decisive. Our response to Jesus Christ makes all the difference. An old tag had it: Either he is God, or he is not good.

The evidence lies before us in the accounts of his life and teaching, in his words of love and mercy, and above all in his death and resurrection. Is this man who he claims to be, or is he deluded, or is he an imposter or an invention? Our reply makes all the difference to our spiritual life. Our response shapes our whole life. It molds our spirituality.

Meeting Christ in the Church

What we think about Christ is not only crucial to our personal and spiritual life, it also affects very deeply the way we think about the community of those who believe in him. Just as there are various ways of looking at Christ, so there are various ways of looking at the church. St. Paul provides us with the famous image of the body with all its limbs and organs. This organic model shapes our praying. When we pray, we pray within this Body. Even when we are utterly alone, each of us is still *a member of Christ*, a limb or organ of one Body.

There are, however, other models of the church. Christians have understood themselves not only as a body but as a people. If we emphasize the church as the people of God, and see this social image as supplementing or balancing the organic image of the church as the Body of Christ, we may come up with a different approach not only to church unity and to the life of prayer, but also to the central Christian teachings. We may, for example, be able to maintain more openness to new expressions and more tolerance for the groping efforts of those who keep trying to understand the implications of Christian doctrine in the world today.

Our understanding of the church and of Christ can become lopsided if it is dealt with as a watertight system complete in itself. It is not a system, but an approach to a mystery, and it is closely related to our understanding of the Trinity and of the Holy Spirit. The church cannot be understood without reference to the mystery of God. The worship of the church is almost always directed to the Father through the Son, in the power of the Holy Spirit. We read in the fourth Gospel: "No one can come to me unless the Father who sent me draws him" (Jn. 6:44). And St. Paul writes, "No one can say 'Jesus is Lord' except by the Holy Spirit" (1 Cor. 12:3b).

It is not possible for us to keep all the dimensions and the relationships theology has come up with in our heads at the same time! We are all given different gifts, as Paul tells us, "by one and the same Spirit, who apportions to each one individually as he wills" (1 Cor. 12:11). "Now the Lord is the Spirit, and where the Spirit of the Lord is, there is freedom" (2 Cor. 3:17).

What do you think of the church? What do you think the church is for? You could work out what your local church really believes about Christ and its own mission by examining what it does. What sort of church do you belong to? What are its priorities, hopes, and expectations?

The Eucharist:
A Place of Meeting With Christ

Let us return to the old priest who by now is taking off his vestments in the sacristy as he recites the final private prayers of the celebrant. He has just presided at the banquet of the new creation and shared the bread of new life, the sacrificed and risen life of Christ. He bows to the crucifix over the vesting table and goes home to breakfast, hoping the coffee will be hot.

The last Gospel with which he closed the service tells again, in theological and poetic language, the story of our going down and our coming up, not only after the pattern of Israel's life, but also after the pattern of the life of Jesus. The Eucharist is also a passing from the old life into the new. Israel went down into Egypt through the Red Sea and through the desert; Israel came up out of Egypt and out of slavery, through the sea of chaos and the desert of revelation into the Promised Land. These are the great Old Testament images of our pilgrimage.

Jesus *came down* into the womb of a woman, into the Jordan at his baptism, into death and the tomb; he came up to share fully in human life and community. He entered into his maturity, and he accepted his calling as Messiah. He was raised from the dead, transformed, and became the source of the new creation opened to all people. This is a theological and poetic description of the deep mystery of the way we grow as human beings in Christ. We use these pictures and images to help light up the way.

The Eucharist retells this drama of human life. It celebrates the passion, resurrection, and ascension, and proclaims the reign of Christ in glory. It is both the great banquet of a king (the Messiah) and also a simple meal shared by friends. The Eucharist proclaims that the ordinary bread is the bread of the Kingdom. It is a sign of a new reality. It is the Body of Christ broken and shared as bread by all for whom it is prepared—all who are called into the Kingdom. The Kingdom is a picture of that remade world in which God reigns. All these images that we find in the Eucharist point to the same thing—our life continually being made new in Christ.

· 11 ·

Meeting Christ in the Bible:
The Fourth Gospel

————

The *last Gospel* (Jn. 1:1–14) is only the beginning of the Gospel according to St. John. But in this impressive "beginning," there is a whole statement about who Christ is. As you read on, you will find the chapter has much to say about the meaning of being human, and about what it means to pray.

St. John's Gospel begins with a general and universal statement, upon the plane of eternity: "In the beginning was the Word, and the Word was with God, and the Word was God." We reach the magnificent climax and proclamation in the words of verse 14: "And the Word became flesh and dwelt among us." From this point on, the chapter opens out in a series of ascending steps as the witness of John the Baptist and the disciples, Andrew and Peter, Philip and Nathanael, reflects a growing insight into the mystery of Jesus as the Christ. The disciples' simple encounter with Jesus takes them as they are, and in him they are destined to become a new people. The revelation of Christ to the world is done in stages. The life of prayer also develops in stages. The deeper we go into the mystery of Christ, the deeper will be our commitment to him in prayer.

In this first chapter of St. John's Gospel, we move from statements on a fairly superficial level to the great proclamation in verse 49, that this Jesus whom we can see and touch is the Son of God and the King of Israel. An even greater claim is made in verse 51, where Christ is described as the Son of Man. This is the climax of the whole series of titles for Christ, where Christ as God is proclaimed as truly rooted in human flesh, in human history.

Jesus Is the Lamb of God: Prayer Is an Act of Sacrifice

John the Baptist points to a real, living individual, a man standing among others. He tells us that this man is "the Lamb of God who takes away the sins of the world." This is an astonishing statement. This man Jesus was to be recognized as God's instrument for the saving of the world. The church understood the image of Jesus as lamb of God against the background of the paschal lamb sacrificed before the ancient Israelites left Egypt. The death of Jesus on the cross is the sacrificial offering that makes possible a new Exodus. Like the mighty acts of the Old Covenant, these final acts of Jesus' life (including his dying and his rising) are also the mighty acts of God in saving human beings from slavery and death and liberating them into the New Covenant. We have already seen that we celebrate and share in these mighty acts in the Eucharist. We also share in them every time we pray in the quietness or turmoil of our own hearts. God's saving power is as surely with us now as he was with his ancient people, and he was with Christ in his death and resurrection.

The church also understood the Lamb as the Servant of God, meek and silent before his oppressors, "stricken for the transgression of my people" (Is. 53:8). So the image of the lamb as both a sacrifice and as a sign of silent suffering for the people is very important for our entering more deeply into who Christ is. What can the picture of Christ as Lamb mean for the life of prayer? Surely it is an invitation to us as individuals and as communities of Christians to wait, to learn to suffer, to be still, and to know that out of the suffering and stillness comes the power of God to change things and, if necessary, to turn the world upside down.

Jesus Is the Messiah, the King, and the Son of Man: Prayer Is a Sharing in God's Promises

St. John the Baptist (Jn. 1:32–33) next reveals to us that the Spirit descended as a dove from heaven and remained on Jesus. "This is he who baptizes with the Holy Spirit." The dove is a symbol of Israel and points to Jesus as the man called to represent Israel, chosen of God, to gather together and sum up her history and to become the new Israel, which would include the whole human race. Just as the Spirit of God moved over the watery chaos of the beginning of all things in the first creation, so the Holy Spirit broods over Jesus the new man at the beginning of the new creation. So this man Jesus takes on ultimate and universal significance. To be *in him* is to be part of the new creation, to be made continually anew in the power of the Holy Spirit. In the experience of prayer, the newness of God keeps breaking in on us so that the mystery of who we are gradually unfolds.

The next witness to the meaning of the man who was "Word made flesh" is Andrew, Simon Peter's brother, who recognizes Jesus as the Messiah, the promised one who was to come to deliver the people of God. Philip's testimony follows this. He gives the man his name, Jesus of Nazareth, the son of Joseph, and anchors him in history on the definite map of Palestine and in the family tree of King David. There is no doubt that Jesus is a real historical person. Nathanael's witness proclaims "Rabbi, you are the Son of God! You are the King of Israel!" He accords Jesus the highest of titles and announces that the promised king of the new Kingdom has come.

All this is quite overwhelming. These images of lamb and messiah are not familiar to us, and it is not easy, at first, to see how they affect our living in the Spirit. The basic thing to remember is that for the author of this Gospel (as for us) there are two vital truths to affirm about Jesus Christ. The first is, as we have seen, that he was a human being, completely and utterly one of us. The second is that he is God, completely and utterly at one with the Father.

The dual nature of Christ as fully human and fully divine is summed up in the claim that is made in verse 51 that he is the Son of Man. The image of the Son of Man in Scripture is both rich and mysterious, for it not only points to an utterly human figure but to one who has the authority of divinity.

The exploration of such words as lamb, Messiah, and Son of Man is an effort to express these two truths about Christ. For the old priest celebrating the Eucharist in our story, who Christ is was expressed in worship: "Blessed be Jesus Christ, true God and true man."

The alarming and wonderful consequence of all this is that in this man, Jesus, who is (according to this Gospel) word-made-flesh, sacrifice, deliverer, revealer, principle of life, Messiah, judge, and king, is found the real meaning of every man and woman. Our pattern of going down and coming up is repeated in his titles as it is in his life. He is the Passover lamb whose blood on the doorpost was a sign of deliverance. He is also the sacrificial lamb, the suffering servant. Jesus is the servant who shows what it really means to be a king. He is also the servant who shows us what is involved in being chosen by God. Jesus is the eternal one, the one on whom the Spirit rests, who enters into his kingdom by the strange way of the cross. And finally, Jesus is one of us.

Jacob's Ladder:
A Vision of Living in the Spirit

In the final verse of the chapter we have an icon of the whole meaning of the fifty verses that have gone before.

> You will see heaven opened, and the angels of God ascending and descending upon the Son of man (Jn. 1:51).

Behind this image lies the story of Jacob's ladder in Genesis 28:12, a ladder that was set up on the earth, whose top reached to heaven and upon which angels ascended and descended. This ladder is a metaphor for the link between heaven and earth, and the angels repeat our basic pattern of descending and ascending, going down and coming up. In the passage in the fourth Gospel, the ladder disappears, and in its place is the figure of the Son of Man himself, upon whom the angels go up and down. He is the link between heaven and earth, between inner and outer realities, the key to what it means to be human. In this figure of Jesus as the Messiah, we find a double movement: one *coming down* from heaven, from eternity, to earth; and the other *going up* from humanity, formed from the earth, to heaven, the place where the mystery of who we are is revealed in all its glory. In Jesus, God and the human race are so met together that they will never be parted.

This, at least, is a vision of our living in the Spirit. But doesn't it sound rather remote and even far-fetched? What does this all have to do with me? I have been sent out from the Eucharist by the deacon and bidden to go in peace, to love and serve the Lord in the world he has made. In other words, we have been given this vision into the true meaning of things, and now we are summoned and challenged to share this vision with others. We have come back to our earlier definition of Christian spirituality as the revelation of and the summons to full humanity. What a human being is, is revealed to us in Jesus Christ. But the revelation brings with it a challenge and a summons to grow in this vision and share it with others.

We have looked at the first chapter of John and asked what is revealed to us about Christ. We have seen that at its heart (verses 14–18) flesh and glory intermingle. God and humanity are joined together. We are made in the image of God, and Christ as the true human form of that image is our basic pattern. He shows us who we are. When we catch a glimpse of who he is, we also receive the power to share the vision. So that, in the end, vision and communication are one. That is to say, we see first and then live by what we see.

We Are Nourished by the Word of God

The Bible is one of the primary places where the Christian vision of reality is communicated. It is, along with the Eucharist, one of those appointed meeting places between God and the human family. In the preceding, we were concerned primarily with vision, with what Jesus shows us of God, so that we might see what it is to be human. In the following, we shall be thinking primarily of how we communicate and share that vision. What are the ways in which we are related to God by the living bond of what is called *grace?* How does God help us to become our true selves?

He helps us when we read the Bible. What do we mean when we say that the Bible is the Word of God? The *Word* in the Bible (in Greek, *logos*) can mean seed, bread, meaning, communication, reason, message, and many other things. It often refers to the utterances of God by which we live as by bread. "Man shall not live by bread alone, but by every word that proceeds from the mouth of God" (Mt. 4:4). For the prophet Amos, the worst kind of famine was not the failure of food and drink for our bodies, but the cutting off of living communication with God: "not a famine of bread, nor thirst for water, but of hearing the words of the Lord." For Jew and Christian alike, the *word* of God is supremely found in the Scriptures. They are an indispensible source of spiritual nourishment.

That is why Christian worship has always been based upon Scripture. The Bible is the great source of nourishment when we say our prayers. In private meditation and contemplation we feed upon that living Word. The Bible is a book with a living Presence in it, and that presence is Christ.

The vital importance of Scripture is symbolized in some places by putting the Bible in a permanent place of honor at the center of the church. Sometimes it is put in a shrine or on a lectern, occasionally flanked by candles or flowers. In our Anglican worship, the centrality of Scripture is sometimes expressed by a *Gospel procession*. When the Gospel is read at the Eucharist, there is often a procession with candles. The proclamation of the Gospel can also be preceded by the threefold sign of the cross on the forehead, lips, and breast, with a prayer that we may receive the Word in our minds, bear witness to it in our speech, and affirm it with our heart and will. This, too, is a way of saying that we believe the Bible to be central to the Christian life.

The Bible Affirms the Goodness of Creation

John the Baptist began his preaching with the claim, "I am the voice of one crying in the wilderness, Make straight the way of the Lord." It is a call to new beginnings, and it speaks to us today. Christian discipleship involves our learning to share in Jesus' self-giving love. Meditating upon this word as we find it in the Bible is one of the basic ways by which we understand the meaning of our daily following of Christ. This meditating on the Word of God takes time, time that needs to be carved out of each day if we take our Christian profession seriously.

In the first chapter of Genesis, the Word of God is creative. God spoke, and it was done. "And God saw everything that he had made, and behold, it was very good" (Gen. 1:31). Everything that proceeds from the mouth of God is very good, including us, his lively images. God the creator tosses out the sun, the moon, planets, and stars, like golden rain. He made and poured out the good things of creation abundantly, joyously, and as effortlessly as a man might speak. As we have seen, in the Genesis account the greatest work of God's creation is humankind, man and woman, "in his image and likeness." We are to trust this image. It is a gift that cannot be taken away from us. We can always return to it, celebrate it, and seek it in others. Christ is to be found in others. "Blessed be Jesus Christ in the hearts of his faithful people."

There is a great deal in an older spirituality that tends to drown out almost entirely any emphasis on the celebration of creation. It was negative towards the material world, as if the things of the earth were unalterably opposed to the spiritual. It was also negative towards the self. The self has taken an awful beating in some forms of Christian spirituality. Much devotional literature has called self-love, self-assertion, self-centeredness, self-importance, even selfhood—sinful.

There is a truth in this judgment—the nub of sin *is* in the self, and the worst of sins, pride, is the setting of self at the top of our priorities. The radically sinful life is one in which everything is harmonized under the service and glory of oneself.

Nevertheless, the human self is a creation of God, and it is very good. Is it not, in fact, the crown of creation, at least so far as the world-view of the Bible is concerned, though who knows what other planets or other galaxies may show us? It is certainly the seat of God's image in man and woman.

When we turn to Christ we find that there is nothing self-serving about him. He does not speak of himself, carry out his own mission, or live or die *for* himself. It is upon who Christ is and what he does that we must concentrate, not upon the abstraction that we call the *self*. Reading Scripture helps us do just that. As we reflect upon what Christ *does*, we learn to follow—to offer the self we have been given as Christ offered and spent himself for us and for the world.

Christ Is the Hammer that Breaks Us Open and the Fire that Burns in Us

The fourth Gospel also tells us that the life of Christ is our light. Insight and understanding are present to us through the Word of God, at the center of our living. We have already seen that the Word of God is like bread that nourishes us. The prophet Jeremiah also compares it to fire and to a hammer. "Is not my word like fire, says the Lord, and like a hammer which breaks the rock in pieces?" (Jer. 23:29). Jeremiah had many problems as a result of taking the Lord's word seriously. Over and over again he tried to be faithful to his vocation as a prophet only to become the target of resentment and rejection. He tells us how fed up he was with this experience and how he rounded upon God, "O Lord thou has deceived me . . . . I have become a laughingstock all the day; everyone mocks me . . . . For the word of the

Lord has become for me a reproach and derision all day long" (Jer. 20:7–8). In spite of himself, however, Jeremiah could not refrain from speaking out. "There is in my heart as it were a burning fire shut up in my bones, and I am weary with holding it in, and I cannot" (Jer. 20:9). Sometimes God's word seems more like bread or like light, but other times it is like a hammer cracking the rock of our hardened hearts or bursting forth like fire in our bones. That is why our praying takes on so many different forms. Sometimes we are quietly receptive. At others, it's as if a battle were going on inside. Sometimes we are silent, at other times we want to argue with God.

We discovered this same contrast of mood when we explored the importance of conversion. It, too, could be short and violent or long and gentle. All of our turnings to God and away from the enthroning of ourselves as gods are prompted by different experiences. The word of God can come as destructive, alien, and threatening. New insight into our secret motives can burn like fire. The birth of new empathy for those we regard as our enemies or our inferiors is accompanied by pain: hammer blows to our pride and complacency.

That is why we find tears, confession, and sorrow are important ingredients of a full spiritual life. Sometimes a new claim upon us can appear as an unwelcome and threatening intrusion—a new friend, a change of job or status, even a new baby entering the family and forcing the rearrangement of life on every level.

This light, this new insight and understanding, painful in its birth, conquers the darkness. It persists, it endures; it serves as a shock absorber and antidote to evil. Whenever we meet injury with forgiveness, the light of Christ shines out and conquers the darkness. We can only do this by allowing Christ to overcome our darkness. It is when we try to do it ourselves that we fail. The light of Christ in us is the power that makes us children of the Kingdom. It enables us to live the life of the Kingdom and to overcome both our own evil and that which others bring upon us.

Christi Is Love
that Always Holds Us in Being

The vision of the word of God who became flesh and dwelt among us is also a vision of fullness. Raymond Brown in his translation for the Anchor Bible ends John 1:14 like this:

> As we have seen his glory, the glory of an only son coming from the father, filled with enduring love.

The two nouns that he translates as "enduring love" are usually rendered as "grace and truth," and reflect the Old Testament's bringing together of *mercy* (the mercy of choosing Israel without any merit on her part) with *fidelity* (God's faithfulness to his part of the covenant). The words *enduring love* point to the content of the *fullness* and the meaning of *glory*. God is love, fullness of love, and this love is glory. *Grace upon grace* suggests the overflowing abundance of the love available to us in Christ, and the image of the Creator effortlessly tossing out the golden seed of all that we need for living life to the full. The characteristic action of God in Christ is liberating, and the wonderful means of liberation is self-giving. This is the saving power of love.

We all know ways in which self-giving can be tyrannical. We have experienced the troubling impact of those who are convinced that their vocation is to explain to us the weaknesses and deficiencies of our faith and practice, to set us right according to their own ideas. We know "the self-giving mother" who gives so much, determines so much, and solves so many problems, that everyone else is forced into the position of being permanently on the receiving end and, therefore, permanently in her debt. Her children become so dependent upon her that they never attain mature independence.

The story of the poor widow, placed in the Gospel of St. Mark immediately before the story of the Passion, points towards and helps us understand the poverty and self-giving of Jesus on the Cross. This, too, provides a pattern for our praying. The woman did what she could towards meeting the needs of those even poorer than herself. She does not do it all herself. It is the combined contributions of the whole community, here a coat and there a basket of bread, from another a bottle of wine, and from yet another a purse of gold, and from this woman two small coins, that the church carries out the command of the Lord to feed the hungry and clothe the naked. We can picture the widow tossing in her little coins with a generous flourish like God tossing out the stars of the sky. Her generosity consists in her willingness to give what she had, not in her determination to meet everyone's needs. After the two coins had rolled down into the offering box with a tiny clink, they were out of her control. They could be used for anything, and no one thanked her for them or sought to repay her. The story suggests that it is worthwhile to give, really give, without strings, the little we have, as our share in the upbuilding of the community and the strengthening of its unity in love, and not to worry about how it is used. This is the way we are to love; this is the way we are to pray—to give the little we have as generously as we can and finding it multiplied by the love of God.

Christ Is True God and True Man

We have come a long way in exploring Christology (the various ways Christians have understood the person and work of Christ). The images we have examined are many and varied (Lamb, Messiah, Word, King, Hammer, and Fire). They are like the facets of an enormous and brilliant diamond. Each facet of the mystery of Christ illuminates in some way the spiritual life of the Christian. Some images will speak to us more deeply than others at various times in our life. The particular image of Christ that we choose will determine and shape our life of prayer. Perhaps, at one point in our life, Jesus as the suffering servant spoke most effectively to our deepest needs. Our prayer life was quiet. We found ourselves going to the eight o'clock celebration of Holy Communion instead of the big service at ten or eleven o'clock. In the early morning we could be quiet, we could be alone. There the man suffering on the Cross could speak to us. He, from his solitude, would enter ours.

At other times, Jesus as King, or as the hero of love, speaks to us. Then we want to be with others, reach out to others. So we see that each facet of the mystery of Christ brings with it its own peculiar emphasis in the life of prayer. Sometimes he brings tears of repentance; at other times a burst of joy. Christ comes to us as servant and as King. He comes always as light in a dark place.

· 12 ·

Prayer:
Sharing in the Life of Christ

In the beginning of this book we emphasized the fact that the opportunity to live as a human being is both a gift and a task. We now see that a Christian (that is, someone who is becoming fully human in Christ) is also a gift and a task.

In what way do we mean that Christ is the center of the Christian life? Why Christ? Why could not any great human being show us what God is like, show how God acts? Why could not Buddha, or Mohammed, or Krishna show us that life demands both acceptance and response, that it is both gift and task? This is a very serious question for Christian spirituality. There is an emerging group of people who are genuinely concerned with the life of prayer, but who are puzzled and even scandalized by the apparently narrow and exclusive claims of Christianity. Do we really need to concentrate exclusively on Christ? Surely we should be open to other traditions? We have so much to learn from the experience.

We do indeed have a great deal to learn from the other religions, but for us the unique characteristic of Christianity is the coming of God into history, into human life. What the great religions of the world teach us is something paradoxical: namely, that we should be open and compassionate towards other ways to God, but that we should also be firmly planted in our own way. Our way is through Christ. This unique way has been entrusted to us. It is this that we must share with others with neither possessive pride nor false modesty.

The appropriate object of our focus, attention, and enthusiasm is nothing less than God himself. We have seen that to be human is to adore, to contemplate (that is, to look at) God, because who or what he is determines who or what we are. Now that is all very well in theory. In practice, as we have seen, we tend to gaze at something less than God. In fact, we'd rather engage in *spirituality* as a task than wait on it as a gift. All our energy and enthusiasm tend to be focused on a passing fancy. This is not because we are necessarily perverse, but because we need something to hold on to. *God* is too vague, too distant, too abstract. Waiting seems such a waste of time. Think of God right now. What do you see? What are you thinking about? Pictures, images, and ideas flood the mind. When you think of God, you may have to be particular. You may, perhaps, think of a holy place, or of a special icon of the Virgin and Child, or of that small evangelical chapel where you first gave your heart to Jesus. You may sometimes think of someone you love. These different things speak to you of the love and the humility of God in a new way that you can begin to understand. You soon, however, get exhausted with *spirituality* as a task, a job to be done. If we are not careful, the life of prayer becomes a treadmill of perfection, a gateway to despair. Sometimes we need to get to the end of our tether in order to be able to receive spirituality as a gift. The gift can come in very strange ways, through a mind confused or a heart torn by conflicting emotions.

We have to be honest with what is given to us in our mind and heart. We offer what we have. Sometimes we give up the idea of prayer because we have unworthy thoughts (not nice stained-glass ones). We imagine that God somehow led a sheltered life! When *spirituality as task*—you might call it *self-improvement*—gets too much for us, we have to stop and begin honestly with our desires, our petty lusts, our own frantic efforts at self-justification, and our longing for *success*.

A prayer life that does not face these things is worse than useless. It is a sham. It can be destructive and even demonic, because it substitutes a sentimental veneer of piety for the real agonies and issues of human existence. The Christian finds the courage to face himself honestly when he faces Christ, personal and particular in the Scriptures, in the breaking of bread, in the fellowship of the church, and in his own heart. Christ's coming is a free act of love. He does not come to confront us with an impossible ideal. He comes to give us himself.

Christian Prayer and the Other Religions

As we have seen, there is a natural reticence on the part of Christians to make an exclusive claim on Christ. Contact with the other great religions makes some of us hesitate in urging any particular claims for him. Certainly the out-stretched figure of Christ on the Cross coerces and bullies no one into submission. That is not the Christian way. Techniques taken from other traditions can help us offer ourselves more and more fully to Christ.

The contemplative techniques from the East, particularly those advocated by Zen Buddhism, Transcendental Meditation, and Sufism, have made many appreciate the calming, focusing, and centering effect of disciplined meditation. Meditation is healing and healthy both for body and soul, but on its own fails to satisfy our longing for love.

It is a pity that the churches, as a whole, have failed both to be in touch with the enormously diverse and rich treasure of Christian spirituality and to teach Christians ways of praying that are centered in the unique gift of God to us in Christ.

There is a great deal to be learned from the Eastern tradition of contemplation, and, insofar as we understand spirituality to be a task rather than a gift, we do have much to learn about the life of prayer from them. There are techniques and skills that we sorely need in order to open ourselves up to God. Many Christians practice yoga. It tones up the body, clears the mind, and opens the spirit. Other Christians have been helped by the insights of Zen Buddhism. The wry wit and gentle humor we find in that tradition can help us to understand a little better the deep mysteries of our own heritage. When spirituality is conceived of as a task, then we all have much to learn from one another. We have everything to gain when we are open and receptive to the different ways human beings have responded to the challenge and the task to become human.

When, however, we view spirituality as a gift, as a given, we come face to face with Christ who is the focus of all Christian hope and aspiration. Spirituality is not so much something we do as something we receive, and what we have been given is the Spirit of Christ.

Prayer Is a Response to the Gift

The Christian believes that God entered space and time, entered our history in Christ, and that this event was God's gift of himself to us. Christian prayer is not, first and foremost, a technique for calming and centering us (although these effects may come). It is living in the reality that God has given himself to us in Christ.

To insist that Christ shapes and constitutes our very being (that is to say, he *is* God) is not to have said everything there is to say. There is much, much more to Christ than we know of him. We know him, but we do not know him exhaustively. Christians have tended to be possessive and proprietory with regard to Christ. We have given the impression that Christ needs a continuous introduction to his world, to his own creation! Christ does not need to be introduced, but to be *proclaimed*. He is not something *added*, something extra. He is present and active now, in every human being, Christian or non-Christian.

The Imitation of Christ

We have already looked at the names, titles, and images of Christ given in the New Testament. We have seen the richness of the struggle to find words appropriate to the mystery. Let us look again at the first chapter of St. John's

Gospel in which we found no less than eight titles for the Christ (the name *Christ* itself is, of course, a title meaning "the Anointed One"). Jesus is the *Word* (vs. 1); he is God's communication to us about ourselves. He is the *Light* (vs. 7): the One who shines in the heart of every human being. He is the *Lamb* of God (vs. 29) ready to give his life for the sins of the world. He is the *Son of God* (vs. 49). He is *Rabbi* (vs. 38), *Messiah* (vs. 41), and *King of Israel* (vs. 49). Finally, he is the *Son of Man* (vs. 51) in total identification with that redeeming suffering servant found in the Old Testament. All these images are offered in this one chapter, and all bear witness to the rich identity of Christ. Because God and humanity are so met in Christ, never to be parted, all these images throw light on our self-understanding.

Much of what we call religion is an act of imitation in much the same way that children act out and repeat the actions and attitudes of their parents.

Religion has been summed up by St. Augustine as "the Imitation of the One who is worshipped."[1] This word *imitation* is very puzzling if we apply it directly to those images of Christ given in that first chapter of St. John's Gospel. Does this mean that we are to be a Word of God, light in the world, a lamb of God? In a way, the answer to this is "Yes!" but an aspiration like this can lead us into quicksand where we easily sink. We are sucked into despair, since it is an absurd vocation for a human being to strain at being God.

What then do we mean by imitation, and imitation in a daily disciplined way? *Imitation* does not mean "copying" Christ in all that he did, but, by prayer, sharing in all that he is. By prayer we enter into Christ and he enters into us. The key word is *discipleship*. We follow Christ, and we share in his life, but we are not Christ. The author of the fourteenth-century *The Book of Privy Counsel* (who also wrote *The Cloud of Unknowing*) put it this way:

> For He is your being and you are what you are in him, not only by cause but by being also, since He is in you both your being—preserving always this difference between you and Him, that He is your being and that you are not His.

This last distinction is a crucial one. How many "religious" people have done great harm in the name of God with whom they have so closely identified that they cannot tell the difference between their being and God's. This is why we so heavily emphasize *spirituality* as a gift. If we understand it as a task, it can easily be mistaken for personal achievement.

Participation in Christ

Imitation of Christ and participation in his life come together when we remember that the very nature of God as revealed in Christ is wonderfully self-effacing. The life that God shows us in Christ is not self-rejecting but rather self-emptying for the sake of love.

One of the great texts of the New Testament speaks to us of the nature of God's being revealed to us in Christ and opens up for us a way into recovering our own true selves in sharing in the outpoured life.

> Let this mind be in you, which was also in Christ Jesus: who, being in the form of God, thought it not robbery to be equal with God: but made himself of no reputation, and took upon him the form of a servant, and was made in the likeness of men: and being found in fashion as a man, he humbled himself, and became obedient unto death, even the death of the cross. Wherefore God also hath highly exalted him, and given him a name which is above every name: that at the name of Jesus every knee should bow, of things in heaven, and things in earth, and things under the earth; and that every tongue should confess that Jesus Christ is Lord, to the glory of God the Father (Phil. 2:5–11, KJV).

Another expression of the joining together of *imitation* and *participation* comes from the pen of St. Bernard of Clairvaux (1091–1153).

> Three principle things I perceive in this work of our salvation: the pattern of humility, in which God emptied himself; the measure of love, which he stretched even unto death, and that the death on the cross; the mystery of redemption in which he bore that death which he underwent. The two former of these without the last are as if you were to paint on air. A very great

and most necessary example of humility, a great example of charity and one worthy of all acceptation he has set us; but they have no foundation, and therefore, no stability, if redemption be wanting. I wish to follow with all my strength the lowly Jesus; I wish him who loved me and gave himself for me to embrace me within the arms of his love, which suffered in my stead: but I must also feed on the Paschal Lamb, for unless I eat his flesh and drink his blood, I have no life in me. It is one thing to follow Jesus, another to hold him, another to feed on him—neither the example of humility, nor the proofs of charity are anything without the mystery (*sacramentum*) of our redemption.[2]

We have quoted St. Bernard at length because he, with all the great mystics, emphasizes the free gift of the love of God in Christ as a saving power. This is the primary fact, the basic given. Our disciplines, our worthiest efforts, do not cause our salvation. Nothing we do can make it happen because it is a free gift. All our dicipline is to be understood as an act of love, a response to the gift.

The drama of our salvation as a gift and the pattern of our discipleship as a response to the gift and the giver (who are one) are spelled out for us in Holy Scripture. Thus, for the Christian, to pray is to be rooted in the Bible.

To Meditate Is to Read the Bible

We have explored the themes of the ups and downs of God's people in Holy Scripture. Let us now take another look at the Bible, but this time as the basic source of Christian prayer. Our entering into the world of the Bible will help to save us from false enchantments. Positively speaking, the Bible is also a source of great power and strength in our pilgrimage. In our sharing in the sacramental life of the church, we are so connected with one another that we are saved from being trapped in the tiny inner world of self-concern. But, as we have seen, keeping our balance between the divergent drives within and the claims from without isn't easy. Daily Bible reading helps us find and keep that balance.

First and foremost, the Bible is central to Christian understanding because it bears witness to Christ. It is a book that is alive. It is a storehouse of memories. One of the best images for the Bible is that of the old family album. It is often around an old photograph album that a family realizes and renews its identity. We pull these old albums out of closets and drawers whenever large families get together, say, for Christmas or Thanksgiving. There are baby pictures, wedding pictures, pictures that stir up sad times as well as happy ones. Looking at the old family album is an important exercise in remembering. It helps us rediscover our roots. It makes us feel that we belong. So it is when we read the Bible. Since reality for us is relational, is convivial, we find out who we are by entering prayerfully and imaginatively into the events, into the lives of those whose encounters with God and with one another in covenant are recorded in the Old and New Testaments.

This exercise of memory, which is so important to our sense of identity, is no retreat into the past. Christians have hope precisely because we remember who we are and where we have been "in the Spirit," with Abraham, Isaac, and Jacob, with Moses and the Prophets, and, above all, with Christ who is God's Word to us about ourselves.

To put it another way, we know where we are going because we know where we have been. Christian spirituality has always been centered in the Bible. In the daily cycle of Morning and Evening Prayer, there is the regular rhythm of readings from Scripture. Christian discipline is the systematic and dedicated adapting of our personal life to that rhythm of the Bible as a living witness now to what God has done in Christ for us. Belief in the creative power inherent in the Bible does not entail our surrendering to a crude fundamentalism. In fact, careful study of the text of the Bible by scholars and theologians does not reduce the Bible to a scrap of paper. In fact, it helps us to believe more rather than less about the Bible by revealing to us more and more of its hidden treasures.

Sometimes the reading of the Bible in a prayerful and disciplined way can be a shocking experience. The dramatic power of the story in which Nathan confronts David with his infidelity can be stunning (2 Samuel 12, especially verse 7).

The Bible read in the context of prayer has the power to expose us to greater realities, to confront us with both glory and judgment, to involve us afresh in the covenant relationship that we have with God and with one another, and to awaken in us the lively person we really are.

Meditation originally meant reflecting quietly on what one read in the Bible. It was not that imageless state of quiet that many mistake for meditation today (which is more like contemplation). Meditation at the heart of Christian personal discipline (for example, in the early Celtic tradition) con sisted of four elements: the reading out loud of a passage of Scripture; the repetition of it in silence; thinking reflectively about it; and, finally, the gathering of it altogether in prayer, or even in discussion with others.

Meditation, in the Christian sense, is essentially an exercise of *memory*. It is the rediscovery of who we really are by diving as deep as we can into the well of a common memory. We prepare ourselves for prayer, for encounter with God, by reading the Bible.

Christian Prayer Is Nourished by the Word of God

To sum up, Christian prayer has always to be nourished by the Word of God. This word to us is Jesus Christ and, in a secondary sense, the Scriptures. The Word comes to us, as we have seen, in our relations with others, in the preaching, and in the Word broken and given to us in the Eucharist. The term used in the Middle Ages for this process was *rumination* (*ruminare*). We are, literally, to *ruminate*, to chew the cud of Scripture!

Christian meditation, then, puts us in transforming touch with the events revealed to us in the Bible; with the central act of the Old Testament, which is the Exodus, with the central act of the New Testament, which is the saving events of Christ's death and resurrection—the New Exodus proclaiming liberty from bondage for nothing less than the whole human race.

Prayer Is an Act of Sacrifice

We need to discover again the central element of sacrifice, which is at the heart of Scripture, if we are to have a lively spirituality of self-offering for the sake of the world. This is an uncongenial idea today, one that suggests self-rejection rather than self-fulfillment. There are, however, positive ways to view the sacrificial Christian way as a way of self-transcendence, of going beyond ourselves. Since Christ is the Way, in him each human being has an ever-expanding horizon.

Our praying is the taking of a stand before the world as a whole. This stand is focused for us in Christ. Sacrifice, therefore, is central to our understanding of prayer.

To acknowledge Christ as Lord and Savior is to live within his sacrifice. We are invited to be a sign of that self-giving love, in the world, and to speak out and act on behalf of our fellow human beings. This cannot be done without self-sacrifice:

> I beseech you therefore, brethren, by the mercies of God, that ye present your bodies a living sacrifice, holy, acceptable unto God, which is your reasonable service (Rom. 12:1, KJV).

Our spirituality, as it grows and develops, will, therefore, be a slow and deepening identification with Christ and his saving power. We are destined to share in the life of the One who is the Word, the suffering servant, the Messiah, the Son of Man. Christian spirituality involves our getting under the skin of the Christian *story*, of our inwardly digesting Scripture as the clue and focus of our identity. We will then see that "what think ye of Christ? and "what think ye of the Church?" are fundamentally the same question.

> "What think you of Christ," friend? When all's done and said,
> Like you this Christianity, or not?[3]

· 13 ·

Praying in the Spirit

We are made after the image of God, and because of this our spirit responds spontaneously to his Spirit. Prayer is precisely this response of spirit to Spirit. We are, as it were, most at home when we are in tune with the Spirit of Christ.

Nothing was ever quite the same after Christ. What he revealed was something about us. Through him we see that we are deep and inexhaustible mysteries related to and destined for God himself. God's deference and wonderful love are shown to us in Christ. The final tag we place at the end of our prayers, "Through Jesus Christ Our Lord," is, therefore, of vital importance. It is the key to a proper understanding of what makes Christian prayer Christian. We are claiming that all our being and doing is in and through him.

As we have seen, prayer is not, at its heart, one activity among many. When we talk about prayer in its broadest sense, we are using a word to describe a person's whole orientation or *style*. We might say that prayer is an expression of the whole person. Christian prayer, of course, is much more than a matter of style, much more than mere personal expression.

The impulse (in all people) to pray is an expression of the human heart towards some kind of end or fulfillment. It is a stretching out towards something or someone beyond us that promises us integrity and a sense of purpose, or that at least holds out to us the promise of an integrity we feel we have lost. The Christian understands that the human being is basically drawn towards God. All our desiring, all our longing, however misguided or corrupt, points to this one end. This end is called in the Christian tradition the *summum bonum* (the greatest good), the *visio dei* (the vision of God). It is beyond words. It is like being in love for the first time. The *summum bonum* and the *visio dei* point to a love affair with God that defies description. This love affair is *through Jesus Christ, Our Lord*.

When we throw ourselves enthusiastically into a relationship of faith and love with Christ, we find our true identity. Then our prayer becomes a movement of love towards God and the expression of our whole person. This is "to know that we are who we are, because *another* is who he is." This *Other* in our midst to whom we are intimately related is Christ. We have now identified this *otherness within* with which we began, as the presence of God himself; Father, Son, and Holy Spirit. It is this *Other* that binds us all together. When we are "in Christ," we are also intimately linked to one another. We are also copartners with everything God has made. This is what it means to be human.

A serious criticism leveled at those of us involved in a Christian life of prayer is that we tend to be very passive with regard to the social and political problems facing the human race. In classical terms this was called *a contempt for the world*. Yet Christian spirituality, which is truly rooted in Christ, has a passion and concern for wholeness, and this continually reaches out to the world in all its misery and pain.

The reason is simple. The Christian sees every human being, and indeed the whole human race, as the Temple of the Holy Spirit. Every individual is, potentially at least, the dwelling place of God. When we begin to see that fact and try to act on it, we realize the fantastic social and political dimensions of living in the Spirit.

There is, however, validity to the criticism that many Christians have made prayer the excuse for withdrawal from, and noninvolvement with, the world. To do this is to misunderstand who Christ really is.

All these criticisms, however, collapse in the light of the lives of those whom the church regards as great Christians. The saints are not, for the most part, antisocial, nor do they deny the ordinary course of human events as the supreme vehicle of meaning. The encounter with Christ always makes us reach out to the world and to one another.

Where are we to turn for guidance? What does the Christian tradition have to offer us with regard to our growth in the Spirit?

Prayer Is a Gift and a Movement towards Wholeness in Christ: It Is an Event of the Holy Spirit

Prayer is something given, and it is given by God, the Holy Spirit. This cannot be said often enough. It is like the air we breathe. It is necessary and unavoidable—simply there for our use. Prayer has something to do with breath, with breathing, with that which keeps us alive. It is something we don't think about most of the time. Many children are, at some point, terrified on going to bed at night, lest they forget to breathe while half-asleep or asleep. Children don't "forget," but the thought of not breathing is disturbing. So to compare prayer with the air we breathe throws light on its meaning. Spirit responds to spirit. God breathes his breath into us. That is what the Spirit is: breath that brings the body to life.

> . . . you take away their breath [spirit],
>   and they die and return to their dust.
>
> You send forth your Spirit, and they are created;
> (Ps. 104:30–31)[1]

A Buddhist teacher once showed his pupil the importance of the desire for love and knowledge. He took the young man down to the river and pushed his head under the water and held it there until the pupil struggled to the surface frightened and gasping for air. "Until you long for enlighten-ment in the same way that you struggled for air, it will never be given you." Our longing for the Holy Spirit in prayer is not unlike our struggling for air in order to live.

The spirit or breath is freely given, and the giver is God. He gives and he takes away. It is not in our power. The Spirit is not something we possess, though we may resist its power or use it for evil purposes. All power, including spiritual power, is from God, and we can misuse it. Jesus himself was tempted to do this in the desert.

So the Spirit is given to us. He constitutes our very being. We are most ourselves when our spirit is open to the Holy Spirit, when the breath of God becomes our breath. Alas, we are not always true to ourselves. To say that all life is spiritual is like saying that all life (to *be* life) is alive. Christ makes us who we *are*. To say that all life is spiritual is to say that all life (to *be* life) is in Christ.

Prayer: the Movement towards Wholeness, Healing, and Holiness

So ours is a movement towards wholeness in Christ, and it should not surprise us that the words *wholeness* and *healing* come from the same root. Our road to wholeness requires a healing of wounds, a binding up of broken relationships, a return to a lost harmony. To wholeness and healing we can add the word *holy*, which also belongs to that same family. The life of prayer is the holy life seen as a movement of healing and wholeness in the power and love of the Holy Spirit.

Converse with God: God's Spirit and Our Spirit

In the Old Testament the Holy Spirit is called *ruach*, which means "breath" or "wind" in Hebrew, and refers most often to a powerful kind of wind that stirs things up. *Ruach* is also used when discussing human beings. It is yet another way of talking about our being made in God's image. Our *ruach* is our likeness to God, our openness to him, and our possibility of communication with him. Genesis shows us the breath of God in bringing the cosmos out of chaos and ordering and garnishing everything that was made. The Spirit–Breath interacts with men and women. The Bible uses homely images to describe our intimacy, our interaction, with the Holy Spirit. Our converse with God is like a conversation with a friend in a garden, or a fierce argument, or an ominous scene in a courtroom. The Spirit of God accuses us, contradicts and confuses us, renders us obstinate. He also comforts, controls, fills, and inspires us. Both parties speak up to one another. Prayer is thus a free interchange: spirit to Spirit.

Another characteristic of the relationship between the Holy Spirit and our spirit is that God approaches the human situation with reference and takes risks as he commits himself into the power of those whom he chooses as his messengers. He entrusts his message to the prophets and leaves it to them to pass it on in their own words and to take the consequences for doing so. In the same way, the Spirit inspires the writers of Scripture, accepting their intellectual and cultural limitations and taking the risk of having his words misunderstood and misinterpreted. When we consider some of the actions ascribed to God in the more savage parts of the Old Testament and compare them with the Gospels, we have some sympathy with the remark of a child, "God does seem to improve as he gets older, doesn't he?"

God's action within Scripture is often a deeply hidden one, conveyed to us through layer upon layer of difficult material—the bloody rubble of the city of Jericho, or the stones of despair in the ruined city of Jerusalem. In other places whole tracts of material, filtered likewise through human experience, are luminous with mercy and loving kindness. God's action, in other words, covers the whole range of human experience. It is not always easy for us to see the work of God, the Holy Spirit, in human events or in the events described in the Bible. When we seek to understand the Word of God speaking to us through the Bible, we need the help of the same Spirit who inspired it. In this way we can sort out a superficial understanding from the abiding truth that lies under the surface. The Word of God is found in Scripture, but we have to dig for it. As the new Catechism puts it, we call the Holy Scriptures "the Word of God because God inspired their human authors and because God still speaks to us through the Bible."

Prayer Is the Holy Spirit Struggling within Us

There are many ways in which the Holy Spirit reveals the Father who sent him, reveals the Son to the world, and reveals us to ourselves. He is always opening things up to us in a marvelously self-effacing way. The Holy Spirit does not point to himself. Consequently, theology has had a hard time concentrating on him. God, the Holy Spirit, is always beyond us, on the move, creating and sustaining all things. The Holy Spirit is the *Go-Between God*, a God who works anonymously and on the inside, as *the beyond in our midst*.

There is so much one could say about the Holy Spirit. From the riches of tradition about the Holy Spirit, witnesses from Scripture, theology, worship, the history of the Church, and the lives of Christians, we have chosen three ways of looking at the work of the Spirit, particularly as they help us to understand our primary concern, which is the life of prayer. They are:

- the working of the Holy Spirit deep within the human spirit to judge, to confront, and to reconcile;
- the illuminating and sanctifying work of the Spirit;
- the creative work of the Spirit within the natural order and within the human community; the Spirit as the universal light.

The Action of the Spirit within Us: to Confront Us and Help Us Grow

According to the Gospel of St. Mark, after Jesus' baptism, "The Spirit immediately drove him out into the wilderness" (Mk. 1:12). Many of us find it difficult to believe that God is capable of tempting anyone, and this consideration has made it difficult for us to understand the phrase in the Lord's Prayer: "Lead us not into temptation." How can we believe that God would lead anyone into temptation? The new translation, "Save us from the time of trial," helps us to understand that in its original context the word *temptation* referred not to our small daily difficulties and humiliations, but rather to that universal and radical testing that was expected to come at the end of the world. It was a dreadful specter, a horrifying possibility. "And if the Lord had not shortened the days, no human being would be saved . . ." (Mk. 13:20a).

The testing that Jesus entered before he began his ministry is summed up for us in the three familiar scenes, those dialogues with Satan, which we find in Mark 1:12–13 (the Gospel appointed for the first Sunday in Lent, in Year B). God indeed did lead or drive his own Son, the Word made flesh, into the naked confrontation with evil itself. God is that tough. He also allows us to be tempted, to the limit of our power and even beyond. It is then that God provides a way through. Of course our temptations are puny compared with Jesus', but they are nevertheless as real and as necessary to us and to our growth and vocation as they were to Jesus. The Holy Spirit does lead us into situations in which we are tempted and that call us from an effort to sort out and to choose from various possibilities, and in the end to affirm the highest good. Our capacities are stretched beyond their limits, as God makes a way for us through the temptation, and we grow through the experience.

God, the Holy Spirit, comes to us in the most ordinary of circumstances. Imagine a morning when, at the Eucharist, the deacon spilled the contents of the chalice all over a small child. Although the child was embarrassed, she was soon reassured, cleaned up, and provided with a fresh blouse from the mission store. Thus equipped and encouraged, she was able to reenter the company of the worshiping community. The deacon was upset also, but she used the occasion to gain new insight into the meaning of her office— how it is to be carried out. She recognized her need to be quieter and more reflective as she administered the chalice and more aware of those who were receiving. "I miscalculated what the child could do." The deacon was also able to pull something beautiful out of a small incident that could have weakened and confused her rather than enlarging her view of things. Grace, the Go-Between God, the anonymous Holy Spirit—are they not pointing to the same divine activity, the activity of healing and reconciliation?

The Spirit Illuminates and Sanctifies

St. Paul speaks about the costly work of reconciliation that goes on in the midst of the whole creation. He describes us "who have the first fruits of the Spirit" as "groaning inwardly," waiting for adoption and redemption. We are exhorted in the Epistle to the Ephesians not to "grieve the Holy Spirit of God" (4:30). In the deep and painful struggle, often over trifles, which goes on within us, we confront the Spirit who can be grieved, and we receive fresh vision as to who we are and who is the God who has chosen us.

Just as the Holy Spirit struggles with us and shows us our sin for what it is, he also illuminates and sanctifies us. He enables us to have a free relationship with himself. He is the Spirit of wisdom who "searches everything, even the depths of God" (1 Cor. 2:10). He makes us understand more and more the gifts he has given us. He interprets spiritual truth for those who "possess the Spirit" (1 Cor. 2:12–13).

The Spirit Is the Creative Energy behind All Things

The Spirit speaks to us through the created world in its wonder and beauty; it may be through natural beauty, like a mountain, a valley, the sea, a leaf, or a shell on the beach; it may be through the sudden impact of a painting in an ancient church; it may be through music, poetry, or someone's journal, or a thousand other things.

In the *Confessions* (Book IX, Ch. 10), St. Augustine

describes a little scene with his mother at Ostia, when "she and I stood alone, leaning at a certain window which overlooked the garden of the house we occupied in Ostia on the Tiber," discussing what the eternal life of the saints must be like. As they talked, they were carried upwards in their spirits, "through all bodily things," passing beyond their own minds' limits to the place where "life is that Wisdom by which all things are made . . . . And while we spoke and longed for that, we touched it for a moment with the whole effort of our heart . . . ."

The Holy Spirit quietly and unassumingly possessed them as they talked and took them beyond their own limitations. They caught a vision of life as it is held in being by the Spirit of God.

How does our understanding of the work of God, the Holy Spirit, affect our life? Think about the human spirit. It is given various names: mind, heart, soul. It is a word that covers all our energies as human beings and can be directed to bad as well as good ends. We are most ourselves when our spirit is open and receptive to God's Spirit.

· 14 ·

Prayer in Christ
Binds Us Altogether

The Spirit teaches us how to pray, and himself intercedes for us. What does it mean when we pray for one another and for the world? Intercession is a puzzle to many people, and it is easy to point out the contradictions implied in much of our practice of this kind of prayer. It is also easy to dwell upon its apparent fruitlessness. Was it selfish of you to pray daily and even hourly during World War II for your two brothers who were in the army? Was it a waste of time for the many people who prayed daily thoughout that same war for the victims of Hitler's campaign to exterminate the Jews? Did any of these prayers matter?

A deeper and more difficult question is about the intercession of the Spirit who "intercedes for us with sighs too deep for words" (Rom. 8:26). Is there a need for asking, for going between, within the Holy Trinity? Does God the Spirit persuade God the Father? Or is this question a cheapening of the reality of mutual self-giving within the life of God?

Or it might help to consider another verse in the same chapter of Romans. "I consider that the sufferings of this present time are not worth comparing with the glory that is to be revealed to us." There are times when we all find it hard to pray for others in any real way. Sometimes we shrink from a realization of the pain of others, and even from the

117

guilt we may feel in recognizing our share in causing it. Sometimes we fail to pray because we lack the courage to share in the grief of someone we love very much. But if we can come to the realization that the "sufferings of this present time" are like a veil woven of sin, misunderstanding, and unfulfillment, which we are powerless to remove, and that the splendor it conceals is gathering there and will one day shine out when the veil is removed, then we can pray for others in hope and in joy. So our intercessions turn to thanksgiving. We can give thanks for all that God is revealing them to be. *The Prayer of Intercession, which is the great mark of the saints, is holding the world in our hearts in the presence of God.*

Our attitude when we pray for others is all-important. It must not be manipulative or bullying. The picture we are given in the Bible is of a little child, receptive and open. In the Gospel, the Lord tells us quite simply that unless we become like little children we cannot enter the Kingdom. In the Gospel of St. John, the Holy Spirit is shown to us as a universal mother from whose womb we must all be born. "Truly, truly, I say to you, unless one is born of water and the Spirit, he cannot enter the kingdom of God" (Jn. 3:5). Prayer, then, and particularly intercessory prayer, requires the open receptivity of children, the quiet availability of waiting.

Intercession:
Reverence for the World Community

Here and there we begin to see in contemporary thinking a developing attitude of reverence towards the earth itself and a new emphasis upon the necessity of dealing with it through its own processes. After the ravages of World War II, an experience that scarred the hearts of men and women even more than it did the face of the earth, a new hope and a new way of appreciating the world began to appear as Christians started to grope a way out from under the debris.

When we reflect on the events of this century (for instance, the widespread slaughter in warfare), we realize the weakness and frailty of human flesh. We can define *flesh* as the human being organized apart from God and centered upon himself. In the same way, we can define the *world* as society organized apart from God and seeking its own authority and fulfillment. Just as the work of the Spirit struggling deep down inside each one of us is directed towards freeing us from the domination of pride and selfish desires and setting us within the freedom of the children of God, so the Spirit works, groaning and travailing deep within every human society, striving to bring forth true community, the *fellowship of the Holy Spirit.*

Like any other community, this fellowship in the Spirit, the Body of Christ, consists of many members, each with its own purpose and excellence. The perfection of any body consists of two things, the fullness of expression of each unique part and the ordering of every part towards a common good. To put it another way, it is the ordering of the many loves of the members under the supreme love of Christ that gives meaning to the whole. We have already considered the principle as it applies to the spirituality of individuals.

The Creator has marked with uniqueness all the living units of creation, from the design of a fish scale or a snowflake to the distinctive whorls that mark our fingers and toes even from babyhood. The sign of life in each tiny, separate, living thing is this uniqueness. When a bit of money was thrust under Jesus' nose with the question: "Shall we give tribute to Caesar or not?" He replied by drawing the attention of his hearers to the image imprinted on the coin. It bore the head of Caesar. So did every other coin. There they come, rolling from the mint, all alike, Caesar, Caesar, Caesar . . . . In contrast to this, he points to the image of God in every person, alive and different in its expression to the one Lord. Coins that are Caesar's may be given to Caesar, but men and women who are made in God's image, each one different, are God's.

Intercessory prayer, therefore, involves a reverence and love for the earth and for all who live on it. When we pray for one another and for the world, we are praying for two things:

fulfillment for each constituent element and the harmonious ordering of the various parts of the common good. Intercession, therefore, is concerned with the restoration of the divine image in individuals and in the whole world community. So we come back again and again to our great theme of our all being made in the image of God.

Intercession:
Reverence for the Diversity of Gifts

In every human group the richness of diversity is a gift of God. We are all one in God's image, and yet each one of us is unique. The perfection of such a community comes from the infinite variety of gifts of service and of working, as St. Paul describes it in 1 Corinthians 12. There are gifts of wisdom and knowledge, gifts of faith, healing, and miracles, the gift of prophecy and the gift of discernment, the gift of tongues and the interpretation of tongues, and all are inspired by one and the same Spirit. All are indispensable, and all are honorable. All are ordered under the most excellent gift, and that is love.

In every situation there are lovely and valuable things, however hidden or humble, to be seen and enjoyed if we can look at them with the eyes of children. It is the Holy Spirit, which was poured in our hearts at our baptism, who enables us to see—to see creation coming from the hand of God and to see one another as individuals and as groups, reflecting the image and likeness of God. The sufferings of the present time do indeed form a thick veil that blots out the splendor from *our eyes of flesh*. It is only by *the eyes of faith* that we can see the splendor of the working of the Holy Spirit deep within. Sometimes it comes to us by the gift of a sudden flash of insight, given when we are most quiet and most poor. This faith and this vision sustain us at other times when we are more aware of that thick veil than of the reality beneath.

Intercessory prayer is a way of our valuing each other with our various gifts and abilities. It is seeing another and simply rejoicing that he or she is. In the end, intercessory prayer is not praying *for* anything. It is rejoicing in others and holding them quietly and lovingly in the presence of God.

Intercession:
The Sharing of the Divine Wisdom

The Holy Spirit is a spirit of wisdom. Wisdom is admired, loved, and desired by everyone. She is described in Proverbs in a beautiful image as a gracious woman inviting all to share in the bread she has provided and the wine she has mixed (9:1–5). But since the world did not accept this gracious invitation, God turned everything upside down and came to us in wisdom as a sign of contradiction, in the folly and weakness of the Cross. Christ crucified is "a stumbling-block to Jews and folly to Gentiles, but to those who are called, both Jews and Greeks, Christ the power of God and wisdom of God" (1 Cor. 1:23–24). This is the wisdom that Paul determined to know exclusively—"Jesus Christ and him crucified" (1 Cor. 2:2).

Wisdom is, therefore, presented to us in two striking images: a gracious woman offering bread and wine to all who come with empty hands to receive her gifts, and a dying man hanging on a cross in the sun. The two images come together in the Eucharist where we celebrate the bread broken and the wine outpoured, and receive ourselves again, healed within and reconciled with one another in the one bread and the one cup, the body and blood of God's son. When the deacon bids us to "Go in peace to love and serve the Lord," we carry that gift and that light out into the world where there are still thick veils of sin and cattle cars of suffering. Christians are those who are prepared to break and share this bread with all they meet. So the kingdom that is to come begins to come now through the breaking and sharing, giving and receiving. "For the foolishness of God is wiser than men, and the weakness of God is stronger than men (1 Cor. 1:25).

The Eucharist is the central place of intercession because there we are all made into a community for the sake of the world. Archbishop William Temple said that the church is the only institution that exists solely for the benefit of those outside it. The Eucharist turns us outward, towards other people and towards the world, because we share in Holy Communion with one another and with the God who made the world. When St. Augustine celebrated the Eucharist, he held up the broken bread, showing it to the people, and said these extraordinary words: "Be what you see, and receive who you are." What do we see? We see broken bread for the sake of the world. What do we receive? We receive the Christ who gave himself in love for us and for the world. As *members of Christ*, we cannot but reach out and hold one another in the Divine Presence. This is what it means to intercede.

Intercession: Sharing in the Work of the Spirit

To sum up: When we pray for one another, it is as if we take one another in our hands and lift each other up and hold each other there in God's presence. Like all forms of prayer, intercession involves waiting. It involves reverence and respect for the one we are holding in our hands. This reverence comes from the knowledge that we too are being held.

We begin with what is closest to us: our family, our friends, particularly those who are sick or anxious. As we pray, the circle gets larger to embrace our local community with its problems and its needs. Then comes the nation and the whole world. It is a natural progression of our holding everything in the presence of God. Often the Holy Spirit demands a response from us to our own intercessions. We pray for a sick friend, and we are prompted to visit, to help care for the family left at home. Intercession that doesn't allow appropriate action to flow from it is worse than useless. It is vain and hypocritical.

We pray for our community, and the Spirit pushes us to get more involved in developing a better school system, safer roads, or whatever. The needs of the world, too, demand a response from us according to our gifts and our temperament. We may be prompted to start by simply getting ourselves better informed about South Africa or Uganda. We may feel called to begin something in our community to point to the plight of the world's poor and hungry peoples. We may be able to bring Christian insights to bear on the foreign policy of our country.

· 15 ·

Prayer in the Spirit: Witness and Waiting

Because we are *members of Christ*, there is no private or special spirituality that we can call our own, no such thing (strictly speaking) as private prayer. There is prayer practiced in private, but, as we have seen, the words *through Jesus Christ Our Lord* place it always within the context and the fellowship of the church. God is Immanuel: God-with-us, and Jesus Christ is the One in whom God and the human race are joined.

The work of the Holy Spirit in the church and in the world is anonymous in that it is characterized by deference, quietness, and reticence. The Spirit, like John the Baptist, points to Christ who leads us to the Father. We use the words *Holy Spirit* to indicate a direct and immediate confrontation with the divine. This is described by the author of the Letter of the Hebrews in startling imagery:

> For the word of God is quick, and powerful, and sharper than any two-edged sword, piercing even to the dividing asunder of soul and spirit, and of the joints and marrow, and is a discerner of the thoughts and intents of the heart. Neither is there any creature that is not manifest in his sight: but all things are naked and open unto the eyes of him with whom we have to do (4:12–13, KJV).

The work of the Spirit may be quiet and anonymous. It is nonetheless powerful. It uncovers things that are hidden. It exposes them. They lie naked and open to the brooding presence of the Spirit. Gerard Manley Hopkins, the Jesuit poet, put it this way: "All things are charged with love, are charged with God and if you know how to touch them give off sparks and take fire, yield drops and flow, ring and tell of him." And John Milton, in his *Paradise Lost*, writes:

> Thou from the first was present, and with mighty
>   wings outspread
> Dove-like satst brooding on the vast Abyss
> And madst it pregnant.

That's what the Holy Spirit does. The Spirit impregnates things with life. Things are so charged with the life of God, the Holy Spirit, that, once we get in tune with them, they give off sparks and catch fire. To pray is to be in tune. To pray is to be on fire.

We should also notice here that Christ and the Spirit are closely related. The Holy Spirit is always intimately connected with and sometimes identified with Jesus Christ. As the Messiah, he is the bearer and giver of the Spirit. Jesus was conceived by the Spirit, equipped with the Spirit, and driven by the Spirit into the wilderness. So, the Spirit is the Spirit of Christ, and by him we are restored to the Father. All things are filled with his Presence. Indeed, in the New Testament, everything is under the direction of the Holy Spirit.

This is the reality that undergirds Christian prayer. Prayer is not, first and foremost, a task, a system of disciplines (as helpful as these can be), but it is, rather, a proclamation and celebration of what God has done. It is a burst of praise in the power of the Spirit.

We Are Trinitarians

The first thing the Apostles did after they received the Spirit was to bear witness to Jesus (Acts 1:8). Christian prayer is, therefore, intimately connected with witness, with mission, with sharing the Good News, because to pray is to be in Christ, to be *enChristed*. To be in Christ is to share in his Spirit. To share in his Spirit is to be a bearer of his Spirit in the world. It is to be an apostle, a bearer of Good News. It is to be an evangelist.

Humanity is recreated in Jesus Christ. This means that we human beings can never be the same again. In Christ a new reality came into the world, a fantastically creative and redemptive energy. We can affirm, through Jesus Christ our Lord, that human destiny is not finally bound up with clods of earth. Yes—we are creatures. We are utterly and completely nothing before the All who is God. Yet in the Holy Spirit we are continually called into being out of our emptiness and nothingness. Indeed, the work of the Spirit (if we would *listen*) is to restore the image of the Blessed Trinity in every human being. What can that mean?

The doctrine of the Blessed Trinity proclaims the unity of God as loving, harmonious, and coinherent communion. This harmony and love is destined to inhabit us both individually and collectively, and the practice of Christian prayer is largely waiting in the silence, allowing the Spirit to get on with his healing and reconciling work. It is diversity in unity: not the unity of an undifferentiated mass somewhere in the sky, nor the diversity of a chaotic multiplicity; neither a flat, one-dimensional unity nor a pantheon of warring spirits. As trinitarians, we find a richer unity through the complexity and diversity symbolized by the relationships of the persons in the one Godhead. This has a profound effect on patterns of human relations. The trinitarian model points us towards a harmony that preserves us as distinct and unique individuals who are yet bound together in community, in common union, in the body that is Christ. As trinitarians, we understand that there is no necessary war between the individual and the community. True individuality builds up and sustains community. The doctrine of the Trinity, therefore, is no purely abstract doctrine, but one with far-reaching, all-pervading practical implications. The Christian, in the community of the church, experiences unity in diversity. Insofar as we can make these distinctions, we can say that the work of Christ unifies. It brings all things together in one act of loving adoration to the Father. The work of the Spirit diversifies by taking the things of Christ and giving them to us. "There are varieties of gifts, but the same Spirit" (1 Cor. 12:4). The diversity of gifts expresses the true catholicity of the church as a free communion of love. We Christians are "the companions of Coinherence" (to use Charles Williams's phrase). We are companions of God, sharers in his divine life. This divine life *coinheres*, that is to say it "hangs together." Because this is so, that divine life makes all reality, in the end, "hang together." *The principle is: we are who we are because he is who he is.*

Christian prayer, then, is the whole expression of a total life, a life surrendered in love to God, the Blessed Trinity. The contemplation (*seeing*) of God in the things he does, and in the things he has made, pushes us into action, into mission, and thrusts us all into pilgrimage.

The Spirit Blows Where It Will

The one thing about God that we humans find difficult to comprehend is his utter freedom. This is because we are not very good at handling freedom ourselves. Our freedom is a freedom of response to God. We are free insofar as our spirit responds to the Holy Spirit blowing through human life. This response of spirit to Spirit is fundamentally an act of praise. "Let everything that breathes (has spirit) praise the Lord" (Ps. 150:6). Thus adoration, praise, and worship are our fundamental stances toward reality, towards God. We are being who we truly are, and being truly responsive, when we praise the Lord! Praise is the expansive utterance of "Yes!" to life. It is like the spontaneous burst of applause that erupts after a musician has managed to combine his sense of inwardness with that of the composer he is trying to interpret. It is an event of the Spirit: an event when the inner and outer realities come together and we catch a glimpse of the true meaning behind all events.

This is what spirituality is about: response to the revelation of God in Christ in praise, adoration, and love. It is that which joins all things together in one harmonious utterance of praise. This praising of God is like breathing. Our spirit breathes back the breath it received in the beginning from the Holy Spirit. Praising is the rhythm of the breathing of two lovers: spirit responding to Spirit. It is *the practicing of the Presence of God* (that is, placing ourselves regularly and consciously in the presence of the One who is always present), so that we too can be freed to be a sign of that loving Presence in the world.

Yet there are dangers. We are quite capable of adoring, praising, and loving, but not all things are worthy or suitable objects of the great "Yes!" This is where discretion and discipline enter the picture. How are we to sort out all the spirits that blow so furiously and seductively in our lives? As we explore Christian spirituality, we may be able to discern the beginning of an answer.

The Holy Spirit does not belong to us nor does it depend on us. The Spirit blows where it will and sometimes comes upon selected individuals, giving them an ecstatic intensity and energy to perform special tasks or meet a certain need at a crucial time. Sometimes, then, the Spirit is an eruptive and revolutionary force.

> And it shall come to pass afterward,
> that I will pour out my spirit on
> all flesh;
> your sons and your daughters shall
> prophesy,
> your old men shall dream dreams,
> and your young men see visions.
> Even upon menservants and maidservants
> in those days, I will pour out my spirit (Joel 2:28–29).

Here is a vision of a mighty outpouring of the Spirit of God on the whole human race. This outpouring is a free act, uninitiated by us. Life in the Spirit is not self-generated, and yet it asks for our cooperation, availability, and response.

Christian discipline is concerned with our response to the gift.

What does spiritual development mean in the context of the creative initiative of God? The growth and nurture of this life, this Spirit breathed into us by God from our birth, requires our loving and free cooperation. Spiritual development for the Christian simply means the ever-widening availability of human life to the work of the Holy Spirit.

Spirituality is not only a condition, a gift; it is also a developing attitude, perceived in the light of this gift of breath. The *gift of the Spirit* covers a multitude of things. It not only means that gift which revolutionizes a person's life; it also means that gift which quietly and unobtrusively sustains and keeps life going. Spirituality is concerned with our being able to see this sustaining power in all things. It is a way of acting on what has been first perceived. In other words, vision always comes before action. Spirituality, from our point of view, is the continued sustained response to the breath of God. This breath of God, as we have seen, can be a whirlwind that ushers in radical change. It can also be the gentle breeze (the still, small voice) that holds us in being at every moment.

Receptivity to the Spirit requires waiting and stillness. Consider the focused attention of a cat about to leap at a dry leaf. The animal is utterly still, poised, its energy concentrated for the great leap. So we contemplate God and the things he has made. We too are focused, poised, ready for the great leap when it is demanded of us. The Spirit is coiled like a spring, always ready. Which way will the Spirit jump? Am I ready? How do I make myself ready to respond? How do I choose which way to go when the command to leap comes?

· 16 ·

God Chooses Us
and Calls Us into
Community

We have looked at Christian spirituality from a double perspective. It is a gift. It is also a task. This has been our recurring theme. In the same way we can see that the mystery of election (choosing and being chosen) has a double edge. We imagine, a great deal of the time, that we are doing all the choosing. We take a look at the various religions, ideologies, and philosophies, and we choose. At least we think we do. It would be nearer the truth to say that the primary reality is that God chooses us. God seeks us out even as we search for him. Truth, in the end, is not so much something we grasp as something that grasps us. It is not something we can organize or manipulate. It is something before which we have to sit humbly. We cannot invent truth. We can only accept and respond to it.

Prayer is primarily a response to a call, to the conviction that every human being is called, chosen, and loved by God. Our life rests with God's initiative even though we'd like to think all the choosing or not choosing were in our own hands. We begin to gain a true perspective on things when we grasp the fact that facts grasp us, when we understand that we are understood, when we are able to love because we

130

ourselves are loved. A true vision of reality is undergirded by what the Old Testament calls the fear of God (Deut. 6:13) and the knowledge of God (Ex. 6:3). This fear and this knowledge involve the realization that God's mysterious and healing presence is behind the pattern of events in human history—the disastrous as well as the triumphant ones. His presence is within our personal histories, too: in our failures, in our disappointments, in our joys, and in our triumphs. It is important to understand that God knows and loves each of us in our failure.

Having affirmed that spirituality is a gift and a movement towards wholeness, and that Christian spirituality is a gift and a movement towards wholeness in Christ, we can now affirm that *Christian Spirituality begins with the sovereignty and initiative of God in our personal and global history.* It is important to say this because spirituality, as we have seen, is often confused with programs of self-help or of personal growth. The basic assumption of Christian spirituality is that we are held in the hands of God. Our knowledge of God rests utterly and completely on our being known by him. Those who are supposed to know him have ultimately to confess that their knowledge of God consists in that he knows them.

> LORD, you have searched me out and known me;
> > you know my sitting down and my rising up;
> > you discern my thoughts from afar.
>
> You trace my journeys and my resting-places
> > and are acquainted with all my ways.
>
> Indeed, there is not a word on my lips,
> > but you, O LORD, know it altogether.
>
> You press upon me behind and before
> > and lay your hand upon me.
>
> Such knowledge is too wonderful for me;
> > it is so high that I cannot attain to it.
>
> Where can I go then from your Spirit?
> > where can I flee from your presence?

If I climb up to heaven, you are there;
  if I make the grave my bed, you are there also.

If I take the wings of the morning
  and dwell in the uttermost parts of the sea,

Even there your hand will lead me
  and your right hand hold me fast.

If I say, "Surely the darkness will cover me,
  and the light around me turn to night,"

Darkness is not dark to you;
the night is as bright as the day;
  darkness and light to you are both alike.

For you yourself created my inmost parts;
  you knit me together in my mother's womb.

(Ps. 139:1–12)

The Community of God's Pilgrim People

In order to enter the community of God's Pilgrim People, we have to leave home, leave things behind, let go of the familiar and the reassuring. It's frightening to be cut off from the known and the familiar. Known and familiar places are refuges and havens when we are wounded in body and spirit. We need these resting places. The journey of the Pilgrim Community can be dangerous, and, although most of us are not called upon to face the terror of violent death, there are battles to be fought, temptations to be overcome. Christian, in Bunyan's *Pilgrim's Progress*, experienced the defeats and triumphs, and the final glory of this great adventure.

We cannot be a community of one. To be a Christian is to be part of a community of friends that supports us in an ongoing life. This is what is known as a tradition: that is, something that transmits life. We need the support of an ongoing life-bearing community, the Body of Christ, the church. We are always in the company of the saints who have been pilgrims before us. While our experiences will never be quite the same as theirs, there are, nevertheless, dangers and glories common to all. We can, therefore, profit from the many experiences that are preserved in that sadly neglected treasure-house of Christian history in which is stored the record of our fellow pilgrims.

Our growth as Christians is always occurring in the company of others. We live in a shared reality, in a common world, in the community of the mystical body of Christ. God has so constructed his universe that we can come to him only in and through one another, as Christ-bearers.

The Christian, therefore, is no unrepentant individualist. He understands that he is part of something bigger than himself. While there is a desperate need for heroes and heroines in the Christian life today, it is not the heroism of a rugged individualism. We need the quiet and steady heroism of a dedicated life. What does a hero do? He has to leave home (the fleshpots of Egypt) and go on a series of adventures. In the crucible of these desert events the Israelites were formed into a people and were able, in the end, to go home (the Promised Land).

The Threefold Path

There emerges in Scripture a threefold pattern for the spiritual life, for our becoming the People of God, the Pilgrim Community. It begins with separation from the known and familiar. It then leads us into the desert of the *un*known and *un*familiar. It is there that we encounter the dangers and the glory of having our eyes opened to a wider vision of things. When that happens we are ready for the third stage—the entry into the Promised Land. This, of course, is only a picture. We never finally arrive (at least, not on this side of the grave). After a while the Promised Land we think we have entered begins to look like the Egypt we've just left. And so we are forced to be on the move again. Just when you think you have finally understood the Christian life and arrived at last at the outskirts of Paradise, something probably happens that makes you fall flat on your face. You pick yourself up and resume the march. In traditional Christian terms this threefold pattern corresponds to the three ways described by the mystics of the Middle Ages:

- *The Way of Purgation,* which is the way of repentance, away from the known and familiar. It is leaving the Egypt of our slavery to the shallow realities of our everyday world.
- *The Way of Illumination,* which is the light that comes to us on the other side of battle, sacrifice, and desert-encounter.
- *The Way of Union,* which is a glimpse of and even a sharing in the abundant, unified life of the Promised Land.

These are only pictures, illustrations, descriptions. But they do throw light on the mystery of our Christian pilgrimage. Why is it that, at times, we feel dry and listless, at other times frightened and empty, and still at others exultant and wildly happy? These are the strange storms and calms of the Christian way. If we learn to become familiar with them, they will seem less strange and less menacing. In fact, they will be seen as the goals and challenges needed to bring us to that abundant life that is freely given to us in Christ.

The committed Christian knows all this in his heart, a heart that the Spirit of Christ has begun to transform through the living tradition in the shared life of the Christian fellowship. The rugged individualist has nothing to guide him except the uncertain compass of his own unruly will and the confusing stimulus of erratic emotion.

The difference between the Christian and the rugged individualist is rather like the difference between the person who can swim and the one who cannot. Both have dived into or been pushed into the water. The Christian, as hopeless a swimmer as he may be, is in the company of other swimmers stronger than he who can help him gain confidence. In other words, the Christian stands within an ongoing tradition. He belongs to a community. He has friends who can help him swim. He is in the company of a great band of strong swimmers who are able to teach others: these are the saints and heroes (both living and dead) of the Christian life.

The plunging into the water is an image of special significance to Christians. It is a sign of our Baptism, a sign of dying and rebirth, a sign of our entering into the saving mystery of Christ. We find it expressed in St. John's Gospel: Jesus tells Nicodemus that a human being needs to be born again:

> Jesus answered, "I tell you the truth: no one can see the Kingdom of God unless he is born again." "How can a grown man be born again?" Nicodemus asked. "He certainly cannot enter his mother's womb and be born a second time!" "I tell you the truth," replied Jesus, "that no one can enter the Kingdom of God unless he is born of water and the Spirit. [Flesh gives birth to flesh, and Spirit gives birth to spirit.] Do not be surprised because I tell, 'You must all be born again' " (Jn. 3:3–7, *Good News for Modern Man*).

The Christian Community
Is Where We Meet Christ

We have seen that a disembodied, otherworldly spirituality is far from the heart of Christianity. The Gospel must be enfleshed. We must therefore ask ourselves the question: Where is Christ to be encountered now? Where can I find him at this very moment? This is no easy question to answer, but unless we do, Christianity quickly degenerates into a nice idea, *a philosophy of life* with no power to transform or recreate us. Admittedly, that is precisely what Christianity is for many people—a nice (or perverse) idea.

We encounter the Christ in the things he has made. We know that we encounter Christ in the Bible. We encounter the Christ in our brothers and sisters—the lively images of him who made us. Christian spirituality affirms that reality is *convivial*. That's a lovely word which aptly describes the Christian life. Convivial comes from *convivium*, which means a banquet, a marvelous meal shared with others. We exist to enjoy life together. One image of the Church is the whole human race gathered around the tale of the Lord as the *sacrum convivium* (the sacred banquet). To be convivial is to be fond of joyful company, and to enjoy a festive occasion.

This is why the theater of our growth in the Spirit is the church, the body of him in whom we live and move and have our being. We could say that reality is *ecclesial, churchly.* This is a dangerous way of putting it, because *ecclesial* could easily be mistaken for ecclesiastical and *churchly* for *churchy.* We are not exulting in the institution as such, but in the fundamental fact that God in Christ calls us into relationship (*covenant*) with himself and with one another. When we talk about the church, we mean it in this primary sense of the gathering together of all the people of God. The church is, as it were, the whole, new, recreated human race in embryo.

A Pilgrim People

Christians are a pilgrim people—a people of the Exodus, and, like the children of Israel, they understand that their pilgrimage always leads them to the desert. This is the Christian tradition. That is to say, this is the Christian way of life. This is the stream in which we flow. Tradition is that which passes on life. It is not a dead thing. It is the life-bearing principle of continuity. We do not have to *invent* Christianity from scratch. As a pilgrim people, we stand in the stream of an ongoing life. In one sense, everyone is *traditional* since he develops his sense of values, his sense of identity by *trading* with others in the realm of beliefs and ideas.

The battles in the church concerning traditions are concerned with criteria. How can you tell which parts of the tradition are essential to the continuance of the common life? There were, for example, dedicated traditionalists on both sides of the painful upheavals caused by the revision of the Prayer Book and the ordination of women to the priesthood. Criteria for discernment: what are they? We look to the Bible, we look to the ongoing life of the church, we look into our own hearts. Tradition, the sharing in a common memory, a common life, involves authority and trying to answer questions like "When is a Christian not a Christian?" "What constitutes church membership?" It is not a question of laying down the law, but rather of calling things, as far as we can, by their proper names. As a pilgrim people, this is enormously difficult sometimes because (as pilgrims) we have not arrived. We are on the move, and while it can be said that we are Christian, we can also affirm that we are still becoming Christians.

The Memory of the Community

The supreme place of the communication of tradition and authority in Christian spirituality is not in philosophy or in law courts, but in worship. In the worship of the church, the most important act is the Eucharist, where the covenant community is gathered for the banquet of the Lord. It is there that we proclaim the death and resurrection of Christ, which, in the power of the Spirit, is recreatively operating now in the drama of our own personal lives, our own history. Our spirituality is set within the context of the People of God (the church) because Christian spirituality acknowledges that human beings, to *be* human, have to live a life of self-transcendence, a life that is always reaching out beyond themselves. It is as if the church proclaimed to each one of us: "You think you know who you are. But you don't. You're a mystery. There's much, much more to you than in your wildest dreams." The church as an ongoing life places you in an infinitely larger world than the private, tiny, splintered one of your own limited experience. When you have *spiritual* experiences, when you are elated, when you feel the terror of death or the joy of love, you are never alone because all your experiences, unique as they are to you, are, nevertheless, shared experiences *in* Christ.

The church reminds us that we are more than our experiences, our feelings, our ideas. We carry within our blood the corporate memory of generations. The tradition of the church is an agent of liberty. It can help us rid ourselves of the cruel tyranny of the present moment and the powerful oligarchy of those who merely happen to be alive now. We, as Judeo-Christians, are at least 4,000 years old.

Much of Christian praying is an act of remembering that the church is the repository and guardian of our common memory. Prayer is the salutary remembrance that God keeps his promises, that our collective history has seen that very same creativity and chaos that we naively believe to be peculiar to our own time.

All our praying, then, is with the fellowship of the church. Let us say again: There is *in Christ* no such thing as private prayer, even though prayers offered in private are an essential ingredient of Christian discipline. We are never utterly alone in our praying. Because the way of liberation leads us into the desert, it will feel desperately lonely at times. Praying within the Pilgrim Community means the painful liberation from many of the things we believed vital for our well-being: it is a movement from our overconcern for self-fulfillment, for self-affirmation, for self-consciousness, for self-awareness to the understanding that true liberty *in Christ* involves also self-donation, self-sacrifice, self-transcendence. In the community of the church we are invited to let it all go. We are invited to be still, to listen to the deeper rhythm, the deeper voices within us and within others. Yet it has always been hard. Tradition is not all that we have said it is. It is often dry and sterile. Authority is not always the liberating force of sane criteria. It is often blind and repressive. Worship does not always communicate life. It becomes stagnant. Communication is often difficult. If we are to see Christianity merely in human terms, we would indeed despair. We need the constant reminder that the church is the Body of Christ.

The Pattern of Life
in the Christian Community

In the Book of Acts the things that bound the Christian community together are perfectly clear. "They devoted themselves to the apostles' teaching and fellowship, to the breaking of bread and the prayers" (Acts 2:42). "The company of those who believed were of one heart and soul, and no one said that any of the things which he possessed was his own, but they had everything in common" (Acts 4:32). So there it is. We may squirm a little, make excuses, suggest that this of course is an idealized picture. Nevertheless, the challenge is there.

To be a Christian is to be part of a community.

- This community is devoted to the teaching of the Apostles. What did the Apostles teach? They taught Christ, bore witness to him, pointed to him as the source of new life.
- It is committed to a common fellowship. To be a Christian is to be in Christ with *others*.
- It gathers regularly to celebrate the Eucharist, the fellowship meal by which the community is constituted.
- Each member of the community is a praying member. That is to say, discipline and dedication with regard to time for private prayer are taken seriously.

Read over Acts 2:42 and Acts 4:32 again. These verses can be helpful in examining our spiritual life and can illuminate our strengths and weaknesses as people and of the Christian community of which we are members. In light of these verses, try to answer the following questions:

- When did I last read a book about Christian life and teaching so that my Christian witness might be fresh, lively, and intelligent?
- Have I contributed all that I can to the fellowship of the Christian community of which I am a member? Do I give up too soon? Do I want to be in control and have my own way? Am I snobbish or contemptuous?
- Do I go to the Eucharist regularly and well-prepared? Is there a way I could go more often—perhaps during the week?
- Do I pray every day? Could I organize my life so that I could find time to be still, to pray for others, and to give thanks?
- How far do I really believe that Christians can share things? How possessive am I?

· 17 ·

The Confrontation with Evil

Every human being, without exception, is a *child of God*. We often, however, use the phrase *child of God* without thinking about what it really means. It is a simple statement, which, on the one hand, points to our covenant relationship with God and, on the other, to our relationship with every other human being. It emphasizes the fact that we all belong together in one family, that there is one reality of which we are part and over which God presides. As we have already seen, this pattern of being connected is best described as a covenant relationship that binds us all to one another and to God.

When we look at the world and at human affairs, we know that it simply isn't true that we are all bound together, that everything hangs together. There is fragmentation. There is evil. There is sin. A life of prayer, if it is to be real, has to take the chaos and fragmentation of human life seriously. When we look at the Cross and wait in its shadow, we begin to see just how seriously God takes our lost and broken state.

Living in Christ means sharing in his life, and that means reaching inward to the lost and broken qualities in our own spiritual lives and reaching outward to those same qualities in others. It has dramatic implications for our behavior with regard to others and, more to the point here, with regard to ourselves. What about our own fragmentations, our own sin, our own capacity for evil? How does an examination of these realities find its place in a Christian's spiritual life? Uncomfortably—but they must be faced if we are to develop an open and freeing spirituality.

The Reality of Sin and Evil

It is good to be chosen, to be within the covenant, under the protection of God, and in right relationship with ourselves, one another, and the world. But when we look at the history of God's chosen people, it doesn't seem so enviable to be *chosen* after all. Even when we accept the fact that God loves us, that he chooses us, things still go wrong. In many ways the world doesn't seem to have improved. Sin and suffering still darken the human scene. Why is this? Why is it that in our actual experience we do not seem to be delivered from the powers of darkness? We still suffer. We still sin, and, in the end, we die.

Sin seems to be a mystery even to God. He says to his people, "Why will you and your people die. . .?" (Jer. 27:13a). It is certainly a mystery to us, but there is no doubt about its reality. It is universally present in human experience. It often seems that it is easier, for most people, to do "evil" than to do "good." Human history is full of stories about evil and laws against it; there are even pictures of it. The Assyrians, for instance, decorated their dining rooms with reliefs showing the torments of their helpless captives and the ingenious cruelty of their instruments of war. Such displays of cruel strength added to the enjoyment of dinner. Why has there been, and why are there still so much evil and cruelty in the world?

There is no answer from the philosophers or the theologians to the problem of evil, but we do find a clue when we examine the mystery of human freedom. There is a close relationship between human freedom and the possibility of sin, and between the knowledge of good and evil and the attainment of selfhood. Nevertheless, the question remains: how do evil and sin live together in a world made and governed by God? Why is it that we who are the chosen of

God, baptized in the new life of Christ, living in the Spirit, continue to betray the best that is in us? We continue to sin.

As we have seen, Christianity is not a philosophy of life. Christianity is the Gospel of God, the proclamation of the good news of what God has done for us in Jesus Christ. It tells us what God did and continues to do about sin. The author of the world's joy, it says, became the bearer of the world's pain. By faith alone we recognize this statement as one of ultimate victory and not one of ultimate despair. The cruelty and evil in the world continually challenge and test that faith.

God Seeks for the Lost

In the Gospel of Luke there is a series of parables about lost things: the lost sheep, the lost coin, and the lost son (Lk. 15). Like most of the parables, these are really stories about God the Father. Under the form of a shepherd he goes after what is lost, finds it, and carries it home on his shoulders with joy. Under the form of a woman, she lights a light, seizes her broom, and makes the dust fly until she finds the lost coin. She then calls her neighbors to celebrate with her. The story of the lost son is more complicated, but the point is the same. The Father had compassion, ran and embraced his son, and drew him back into the circle of family acceptance. He points out to the elder son, whose nose is out of joint, that what he does is fitting because the brother who was dead is alive, what was lost has been found. All of these parables help us understand that God is at work at the heart of things, actively seeking the lost in order to restore them to their rightful place within the community of the Covenant.

Just as our efforts to understand the mystery of evil never meet with success, so in our own experience there is an element of mystery in the fact of our sin and our sinfulness. We know it is there, but we find it difficult to focus upon it. One of the English mystics said, "Sin is a lump," and maybe this is why it is hard to see. It is, like most lumps, dull, uninteresting, unmemorable.

The Christian, therefore, cannot explain this dark lump

which we call sin. It is there. It is real, just as our sense of being lost is real—even though we cannot always explain how and why we strayed and were lost. The God whom Christians worship takes away the lump of sin and recovers the lost. One of the ways in which God restores and forgives us is through a sacrament, an outward form of an inward and spiritual gift and grace.

Sacramental Confession

About a hundred years ago, under the influence of the Oxford Movement, the Catholic Revival in the Anglican Communion rediscovered the practice of sacramental confession. A series of books and pamphlets appeared offering concrete instruction on self-examination, confession, amendment, absolution, and the acceptance of a penance. No doubt the old priest whom we thought about in connection with *the last Gospel* used this literature in his own life and in his pastoral work with others. It is likely that if you made a *first confession* you remember it vividly. It usually makes a deep impression, especially on young people.

This rediscovery of confession was very important to the Anglican Communion, but like many good things, the idea of *making our confession* became distorted in the minds of many and was considered with only one point of view or school of thought. To make our confession was considered *High Church*, or even Roman Catholic. Nowadays, the sacrament is perhaps better understood, and understood in a way that makes it available to people from all sorts of traditions and backgrounds. Perhaps it is time for us to take another look, or even a first look, at the sacrament of Reconciliation, as it is now called.

There is a danger of our concentrating so much on our sins that we lose sight of the forgiving and restoring love of God. There was a time when people made great lists of their sins and became involved, perhaps too involved, with scrupulous bouts of self-examination. People today are either totally confused about what sin is or, worse, are convinced that they are not really sinful at all. Regular self-examination (even to the point of making a list of faults) can be very helpful provided we keep in mind the purpose of such an exercise. It should be done for the sake of honesty and self-knowledge—not for the sake of dwelling morbidly on our sins or egocentrically on ourselves.

Making a List of Our Sins

Making lists of sins can be useful as long as we understand that they cannot *solve* problems. But they do help us to see more clearly who we are and what things we need to face about ourselves. At different times in our lives different sins rise to the top of our lists. The traditional categories of *uncharity* and *unchastity* figure prominently in the lists of many people—perhaps because *uncharity* is a vague and general concept and sexuality has long been associated with sinfulness. The latter idea is a gross misunderstanding, but such misunderstandings die hard.

Much of our sinning isn't altogether deliberate. Very few of us work out a well-thought-out program of wrongdoing, although sometimes our sins are premeditated. We tend to sin, to betray the best that is in us, in that twilight area between conscious deliberation and half-conscious reaction. One of the problems with the traditional making of lists was that of sorting out which sins were really deliberate and which were not. Modern psychology has done a great deal to illuminate the complexity and subtlety of our sinning. Lists that reveal the true nature of things are harder to make because more and more is being revealed of the hidden depths of the human spirit. The problem of telling what is *deliberate* is always difficult. We don't often deliberately look God squarely in the eye and say, "I know this is sinful, and I'm going to do it." We know that there are all sorts of less brazen ways of sliding, backing, and dodging into sin.

Another problem has to do with the sin of anger. What are we to do with our anger? According to the writers of pamphlets on confession, any expression of anger, however trivial or justified, was almost certain to be sinful, including *critical thoughts*. But how can we assess a situation realisti-

cally without criticism? And if every expression of the
passion of anger is always a sin against charity, why is it part
of our human equipment? The same is true of sexual desire.
If all expressions of it are sinful—except between the married—how will anyone ever grow up, and why are most
humans so prone to sexual desire for much of their lives?
Freeing ourselves from false or exaggerated evaluations of
our conduct and finding out the root and cause of our real
sinfulness, lostness, and brokenness is not always an easy
matter. We can take a good look at ourselves and make our
list, but more often than not, it takes another person (a
friend, a guide, a spiritual director) to bring us face to face
with what is really going on. Without the help of a friend or
guide, the making of a list can be depressing and discourag-
ing. A mere list can be the sign of our continual failure to live
up to an impossible standard.

Sin lists can also give us a damaging and unrealistic way of
dealing with our feelings. We look at our list, written or
unwritten, and find, for example, sins of resentment or lust.
What do we do? We tend to drive them underground and fail
to see that they are signs of something good working in us.
The good has been misdirected and distorted, to be sure, but
until the resentment and misdirected desire are brought to
the light of day, they are left to fester and corrupt. They
cannot, of course, simply be unloaded in a damaging way on
others. They have to be accepted as our own. The church,
over the centuries, has provided an environment in which
we can honestly face up to ourselves, in the celebration of the
sacrament of Reconciliation. Lists, made for the sake of
honesty, can allow the healing strength of forgiveness and
acceptance to flow.

The Reconciliation of Penitents

For the first time since the Reformation, the sacramental rite
of confession has been restored explicitly in the new Prayer
Book, under the title *The Reconciliation of a Penitent* (p. 447).
(The 1928 Prayer Book provided only implicit justification for
confession.) A rubric now provides for a variety of settings.

The priest may sit on one side of the altar rails and the penitent kneel on the other, some private place may be used where the penitent kneels and the priest sits, or where the priest and penitent sit facing each other "as for a spiritual conference." Two forms for the confession are provided, and a clear statement is made about the seal of confession binding upon the confessor. It is in such a setting (sitting facing the confessor) that many people have begun to find a new and more helpful way of approaching the sacrament of reconciliation.

Stages of Penitence

Falling into sin is like falling into a black pit. We have seen that this experience of falling characterizes our Christian life. Another way to understanding the mystery of human sin is by looking at what we do when someone close to us dies, or when someone is told that they do not have long to live. Sin is like bereavement, and our reactions to it often follow the same pattern as those of the bereaved or the dying. The first stage is denial. We refuse to acknowledge that we have sinned at all. Justifications and excuses, most plausible and most fair, drown out that other small voice that tries to suggest that perhaps something is wrong. The next stage is anger. As we succeed in transferring our negative feelings from ourselves to some other handy subject, perhaps the person closest to us, or a rival, or a representative of our least-favored group, we become angry with others and sorry for ourselves. The first tears of the penitent are often tears of self-pity and frustration.

The transition from anger to grief is crucial. It is at this point that we begin to face the truth about ourselves. Here grief, real penitence begins. What is penitence? It is taking a long look at who we are and facing honestly what we see. It is the willingness to turn to God and be healed.

Hitherto we have hesitated at the entrance to the dark pit. When we begin to see that in some way, however obscure it may be, we are in the wrong, we begin to enter the reality of what we have called the black pit. As we go down the stairs into the darkness of humiliation, perhaps to remain there for a long time, a new light eventually begins to dawn.

Prepare to Make Your Confession Now

Many of us are nervous about sharing our deepest thoughts and talking about those acts of which we are deeply ashamed with others. It might help you prepare for confession if you read one of the famous New Testament stories about separation and reconciliation: the Prodigal Son (Lk. 15), the woman taken in adultery (Jn. 8:3), and the woman drying Christ's feet with her hair (Lk. 7:36), and meditate on the one which speaks to you.

What does it tell you about God? What does it tell you about yourself? Now make a list of things: What habits, characteristics make you unhappy? What sort of things do you do (have you done) to make you feel sad or ashamed?

What does the list look like? Is it honest? Is it as true as you can make it? Is there anyone whom you trust enough with whom you could share this list? Sharing such things with someone we can trust not only lightens the burden but also brings to bear another point of view. Perhaps we have a tendency to dramatize and exaggerate some of the items on our list. A friend can help us "test for reality." A guide can also point out to us where we might be ignoring our playing down something that we should take more seriously.

More importantly, "sharing our list" with someone is a way of saying "sorry" not only to God but also to the community. We not only sin against God, but also against one another, and telling someone we're sorry can be a helpful way of understanding what sin is. The priest, a sinner like us, is the appointed representative of the community against which we have sinned. The priest is there to celebrate the healing and forgiveness that is proclaimed at the heart of the sacrament. It is his or her privilege to be the bearer of good news.

Read over the two forms of Reconciliation in the new Prayer Book. Perhaps something has been burdening you for a very long time? The sacrament is an ever-present invitation from God through his covenanted community, the church, to get rid of that burden, to begin life all over again. In the Eastern church, confession is called *the mystery of the second Baptism*. That's exactly what it is: the opportunity, no matter who we are or what we've done, to begin again. The time is always now.

· 18 ·

Rhythm and Rule in the Christian Life

In Christ we are forgiven and accepted. We are loved. This is good news. What happens when we accept this good news of forgiveness and reconciliation? We begin to view life in a new way. Everything is seen from the perspective of the wonderful fact that we are restored and accepted in the power of the Spirit. Because the Gospel of reconciliation is preached to a broken world, we can expect to meet danger and excitement, terror and hope. We can expect to enter the mystery of the death and resurrection of Christ happening *now*.

Death and resurrection are like the two poles of the Christian's world. Indeed, there are many such polarities in the Christian life: sorrow and joy, tears and laughter, solitude and intimacy. One such polarity describes the basic rhythm of Christian spirituality. It is best described as two alternating movements of expansion and concentration. The movement of *expansion* involves the widening of our horizons, the breaking open of our vision. *Concentration* is the focusing and harnessing of our energies and powers in the life of the Spirit. The trouble is that we cannot do two things at once. We cannot expand and concentrate at the same time. That is why Christians often seem at cross-purposes, because people are at different points of the rhythm. One person may be struggling in his or her spiritual life within the dark shadows of the Cross, while another feels healed and bathed in the light of the Resurrection. The former can seem pessimistic and dour to the latter, while the latter can appear frivolous and trivial to the former. Both have caught a glimpse of the vision of Christianity. Each needs the other to keep his vision whole.

There is the very ancient story of a great tree that stretches from earth to heaven. One side is living. The other side is dead. It is said that we go through life by climbing upwards around the trunk of the tree, first on the dead side, and then on the living side until we reach heaven. This is only a picture, but a significant one for Christians who see life as rhythm centered around the mysterious life-giving tree of Calvary.

Expansion and concentration, then, are the two movements of the spiritual life. This rhythm brings with it both joy and pain. The movement of expansion is when we begin to experience, for example, a painful and guilty awareness of the oppressions within our society, of the putting down of persons of other races and creeds, or of the opposite sex. We suddenly see things in a new way. God's light shines on everything and shames us. How could I have been so blind, so unimaginative, so insensitive? This process of growth of awareness is often painful. We not only have an expanded view of the world, but we become more aware of the aggressive, exploitative, and oppressive drives in our own hitherto unconscious lives. But there is a good side too. A heightened awareness of the beauty and vulnerablity of the earth and of all natural things is beginning to change the way we live and the way we pray.

As we have seen, depth psychology, at first hand in psychotherapy, or by many secondhand routes, through reading, conversation, television, movies, plays, helps us to recognize some of the dark forms crouching in our own unconscious minds. We are exhorted: "Have them out in the open where you can deal with them." Only when they enter the sphere of our conscious life, it seems, can they be disarmed and converted into friends. Only then can their psychic energy be available to us for creative use.

Such a transformation requires us to give ourselves to the disciplines of the second of the two basic movements: focus and concentration. Without this second movement, which balances the expansion of vision, we are in danger of surrendering to whatever comes into our minds at a particular moment, and even of believing that this surrender is freedom. As Christians, we are to focus on the death and resurrection of Christ.

Entering the rhythm is costly. This is because we have a strange double nature. It is manifested in all those polarities we mentioned earlier. We are capable of sharing in the life of God himself, and yet we remain vulnerable, dependent, mortal, and inconstant. We are marked for death and for divinity at the same time.

When we accept the trinitarian presence within, it pervades all things and uncovers the dark recesses of sin and evil in the world and in human hearts. The light and love of God burn us before they transform us. We become aware of a wounded and crucified Presence that gets to the very root of our voluntary and involuntary evil. This Presence enters us, suffers with us, and opens in us the way of escape. In Christ, God invites us to share in his suffering for the sake of the world. This is what is meant by the strange Christian command to "take up our cross." It is then that we find the cross to be full of healing and reconciling power.

Healing and reconciliation are at the center of the spiritual life. What is amazing is the reticence, gentleness, and deference of the work of God, the Holy Spirit, in human life. We are never forced or coerced. We are invited, summoned, challenged to share in God's creative work. We are co-creators with God of our own lives. This is an awesome responsibility and a stupendous privilege. Healing and reconciliation are part of that marvelous cooperative enterprise by which we become more and more what we are meant to be: children of God and brothers and sisters to one another.

We do, however, fall again and again into sin, even after our most generous repentance and heartfelt efforts towards amendment. This is not due to any squeamishness or impotence on the part of the Lord, who, merciful and mighty, unshocked and undismayed, never forsakes us. It is part of the mystery of sin that we do go on making mistakes, wounding and failing one another, even after we have experienced Reconciliation. The rhythm of the Christian life helps us to move on, knowing that greater than the mystery of sin is the mystery of God's love.

The Rhythm of the Desert

As we have seen, one of the reasons we fail one another and fail to grow ourselves is our inability to deal with the desert. The children of Israel, newly taken into the Covenant, faced a forty-year journey in dry and barren country. Jesus, after his baptism, headed out into the desert of temptation. The rhythm of the Christian life seems to follow this pattern. It is a peculiar fact that when we have been converted, when we have heard God's call, when we have received the gift of reconciliation, we are "driven into the wilderness." The lessons we are set there are painful, protracted, and searching, but they must be learned if we are to pass beyond the introductory and adolescent stages of the Christian life. The refusal to enter the desert when we are invited to at various stages in our spiritual development can lead to problems later on. Middle age, for example, can be a notoriously monotonous and disillusioning time of life. It is all too often a slow, steady decline as we stagger from disappointment to disappointment, as we slide from disillusionment into despair. We can end by abandoning the whole enterprise, either in an adolescent act of rebellion and apostasy, or in a slow and gradual breakdown of all our relationships. Even our closest and most intimate relationships become dry and bitter.

Most human relationships are based on patterns of negotiation and arbitration. What we imagine as *love* is sometimes little more than a mutual agreement not to interfere. It is contractual, not unconditional. The essential covenant relationship we have with God, with the world, with one another, and with ourselves is trivialized and diminished by our bargaining procedures and our damaging inability to be lovers. Intimacy in the end is denied us. Friendships grow cold, marriages die. We all strike for more pay, for more strokes. True relationships depend on a disarming act of self-giving, of self-surrender, of self-sacrifice, and very few of us seem capable of this. Most of us opt for the kind of related-ness based on sheer force: money, prestige, machismo, or whatever skill, charm, asset, or gift we have, for the purpose of manipulation and control. We tend to develop those qualities that are most salable, most marketable, because we live in an age where we have to make ourselves sufficiently attractive so that someone, somewhere will want to "buy" us.

The mystics write about the experience of the *dark night* as a time of dryness and temptation, daunting but necessary as a purification from deep-seated spiritual ills. The desert is a symbol we have used to point to all these experiences: including not only our ordinary passing temptations to slackness and pettiness, but also those experiences of long-drawn-out depression and discouragement and of total abandonment by God.

There are no signposts in this desert. The shifting sands cover our own footprints as well as those of the travelers who have gone before us. Sometimes we seem to be sitting in an impenetrable fog. We hear a voice which says "Turn! turn! turn!" and we cannot turn. All ways look alike. We labor this point because it is in the recognition of our hopelessness that hope is born, that rescue comes.

The mystics again tell us that our only safety lies in acceptance, in dwelling in lostness and emptiness, trusting in the God of whom we have lost track. The Spirit who prays within us stands guard over the fantastic open emptiness of our heart, seeking to prevent the space within being filled up with anything other than God.

The *desert experience* teaches us that no one and nothing can fill the vast emptiness within. Only God can fill and fulfill us. It is one of the tragedies of human relationships that we demand that our lovers and friends play the role of God for us. We are destined to disappoint one another because no one can bear the burden of divinity. The glories of human intimacy and love, therefore, elude us. No human being, however much we love him or her, can fulfill our deepest longing for communion. No lover, family, or community, however important for our well-being, can satisfy all our longing for healing, for wholeness, for holiness.

In the desert we come, with agonizing slowness, perhaps, and many setbacks, to be still. Eventually we learn to surrender ourselves more deeply to the sovereignty and initiative of God. He will bring us through the fog and the darkness of the abyss of our own emptiness to a new perception of our relatedness to himself, to others, and to the whole created world. We learn anew that the human race is, in essence, one reality. There is a solidarity about human beings. We are made of the same stuff. We are invited to adopt a compassionate and contemplative attitude to our brothers and sisters, because it is a recognition of what we basically are: God's children.

Food in the Desert

A balanced spiritual life will always be deeply committed to the daily reading of the Bible and the regular attendance at the Eucharist. It is through the Bible and through the Holy Communion that we begin to live out the mystery of what it is to be chosen. These twin pillars prevent us from falling into arrogance and pride with regard to our election. Our being chosen is for service. Our being chosen is to follow the way of the Cross. Our being chosen is to be a sign of the rising and risen life of Christ.

Christ in the sacrament of his Body and Blood makes us who we really are by making us his own. We *are* the Body of Christ. St. Augustine reminded his own congregation of the heart of the Eucharistic mystery by saying: "It is your own mystery which is laid upon the altar. . . ." When we go to the Eucharist we are not mere spectators. We receive Christ, and we receive our broken and healed selves back. When we say "Amen!" after the priest has said "The Body of Christ, the Bread of Heaven," we are saying "Amen!" to ourselves too. Our brokenness is taken up into the broken bread, and we can begin again.

Think about the Eucharist for a moment. We need the stillness and the silence to allow us to see and enter into its true meaning. Pause before you eat the bread next Sunday. Look at it in the palm of your hand. It is the simple basic element of life. It is Christ. It is you. Remember that command of St. Augustine, which we have already mentioned:

Be what you see
Receive who you are.

"Be what you see. . . . Receive who you are!" These are stunning words. What do we *see* when we look at the consecrated bread in our cupped hands? The bread is a sign of covenant, of promise, and of love. It is broken bread that shows us the cost of covenant. Can we *be* that? A sign of costly covenant? Can we receive it?

A Rule of Life

We can now begin to see something of the shape of the balanced spiritual life. What are its essential elements?

- Time: We need the courage to carve out *a desert place* in our hearts as a daily meeting place with God.
- Adoration in Silence: The most important prayer is in the deep silence and stillness of the human spirit.
- Intercession: Praying for others (or better, praying in and through others) comes naturally when we make ourselves available to God in silent prayer. In him we become more and more available to others in the world. Their needs, their joys, their hopes become ours.
- Service: Christian prayer always expresses itself in some form of service. Christian service is the spontaneous

overflow from our intercessions. When we dare to pray for others, things begin to happen.

These four basic elements in the Christian's *rule of life* are continually tested, challenged, and stretched by the reading of the Bible, by the participation in the Eucharist, and by sharing in the fellowship of the Church. It is all part of our living the mystery of being chosen. We live it out by telling the story of what God has done in the Bible. We live it out by telling the story of what God is doing in our own pilgrimage. We live it out by celebrating the joy and power of the new life in Christ as we play out the drama of the Eucharist.

The Importance of Solitude

Christian solitude, which is an essential part of a balanced spirituality, is not, therefore, an escape from other people nor from the world, its problems, and its miseries. Christian spirituality means engagement with the world and its people. Christian solitude is preparation for, and indeed part of, that engagement.

It is often difficult to find the time to be alone. Busy schedules, family life, and just general coping prevent us from taking the time to be quiet. Even when we do find ourselves with a few minutes to spare, the temptation is to fill up those precious moments as quickly as possible.

Are you the sort of person who finds it easy to sit quietly all by yourself? Or are you a person who finds prolonged periods of solitude unbearable? Solitude is a whole world apart from loneliness. Loneliness eats away at us and leaves us tired, disillusioned, and exhausted. Solitude (the ability to be still with oneself), on the other hand, nourishes us and leaves us refreshed, open, and renewed. Solitude enables us to be intimate with others without the desire to possess and control them.

Which part of the Tree of Life are you climbing at the moment? Do you feel yourself caught on the dark and dead side, or are you enjoying the color and shade of the living trunk? Do you see your life beginning to take shape in the rhythm of the Holy Spirit: the rhythm of death and resurrection, of sorrow and joy, solitude and intimacy?

Is there someone with whom you could discuss this? Perhaps you need to withdraw for a while to gather strength for whatever God is preparing for you? Perhaps the time has come when you should seriously think about making a retreat? A long weekend in a quiet place is a wonderful way in which to refresh the spirit.

Making a Retreat

Making a retreat isn't as easy as it sounds. Many people feel the need for a quiet few days away, but few actually get to the point of arranging their lives so that it can happen.

Some still think of a retreat as something for monks and nuns, or at least for people who are more "catholic" within the Episcopal Church. It is true that retreats have always been a popular and important part of Catholic spirituality, but most people, from whatever part of the religious spectrum encompassed by Anglicanism, would benefit from a few days respite from their busy routines.

The really hard thing is deciding to do it. It often takes an enormous amount of organization to clear a long weekend. Those with families have to see that the children are taken care of and, what's worse, come to the realization that the family is perfectly capable of managing very well without them for a few days.

Retreats are often held in quiet places in the country with spacious surroundings. The schedule is such that there is plenty of time for walking and sleeping. Retreats usually begin with supper on a Friday evening and end some time after lunch on the Sunday to enable people to get home in plenty of time to prepare for the working week.

Many retreats are held in religious houses. Episcopal religious orders are usually marvelous at providing an atmosphere of refreshing silence, which isn't overbearing or threatening. There is usually a retreat conductor who is often a priest (though not always), who gives one, two, or three meditations a day and who is available for counsel, conversation, and confession.

The most important part of a retreat is the silence that usually begins to deepen and sink in after twenty-four hours. At first the silence is only on the surface. Inside we are still frantically busy and very noisy. It takes at least a day for our motors to slow down and simply to idle. It takes discipline and not a little courage to allow that to happen.

We don't go on a retreat to solve any problems. We go simply to be still, to be quiet, to wait on God. When we do slow our motor down, when we do simply idle, then God can reach us. Our problems don't go away after such a weekend. They do, however, look different because they have been placed in the expansive setting of the loving Presence of God.

Part Three

———

MAPS, GUIDES, AND TREASURES

———

· 19 ·

Maps for the Journey:
Types of Spirituality

There are wonderful resources at our disposal that will help us to grow in the life of the Spirit. Maps are provided by the things that God has made (in Creation), and we can gain perspective and sense of direction by examining regularly and thoroughly the various ways in which God has dealt with his people (in the Bible). There are also the great traditions of spirituality which can nourish us. Anglicans, at their best, have appreciated the insights of the other great traditions of spirituality—Protestant, Catholic, and Ortho-dox. There are many guides and many paths, and there are many glories of our Christian heritage to be uncovered. If we're willing to be patient and dig down deep into things, we shall find unexpected treasures.

There's a story of a poor man who had a very rich friend. The rich man wanted to help his friend, so one day he placed a fabulously expensive diamond in the poor man's pocket as he lay sleeping. The rich man slipped away unnoticed. When the poor man woke up he went on living as he had always done, from hand to mouth with barely enough provisions for himself and his family. Eventually the rich man came to visit his poor friend after many years of traveling and was shocked to see him still as poor as ever. "What did you do with the diamond I left with you?" "What diamond?"

replied the poor man. "Why the one I left in your pocket!" At that the poor man reached into his pocket and found the diamond. Spiritually we are like that poor man. We go around in spiritual rags when all the time we carry about on our very own person a great spiritual treasure.

Most people know little about the treasures of our shared Christian tradition. Many of us are also fascinated with Eastern ways of spiritual growth. If we add to the ignorance of our own treasures our fascination with someone else's, the possibility for genuine spiritual growth is greatly diminished. The fourfold pattern of covenant with God, with the world, with others, and with ourselves is hard to see when all of our values seem to be in flux. Many appear to have lost the ability and even the will to relate very deeply on any level. We need to recover a sense of our roots if we're to relate to one another as mysteries.

Why Maps Are Necessary

When the fundamental relationships that bind us to God and to one another are threatened, the possibility of disintegration and chaos looms large on the horizon. Chaos, however, is unendurable, and we look for something or someone to give us a clue as to how we may best combat it. We look for a map, for a guide. At our deepest level we understand that forms and structures of some kind are an important condition of true freedom. The sad thing is that we sometimes prefer relationships with God, with the world, with others, and within ourselves that imprison rather than free us.

The total absence of structure is unendurable. That is why there are new forms, new fundamentalisms, gaining popularity in our culture. They provide maps and sets of instructions. We long for answers and feel unable "to love the questions themselves," as Rilke bids us.

We live in a wild and violent age. In our cities aimless and gratuitous acts of violence are committed out of the terrifying inner emptiness and boredom that haunts young people who are jobless and without hope for their own future or the future of our society. They feel lost, lonely, and afraid. The risk of rape or mugging is not only present in New York and Chicago. It stalks our suburbs and infests many small towns. Yet, at the same time, there is a fantastic expectancy, an expanding vision, a widening horizon exploding in the corporate consciousness abroad in the land.

We live in an age of great fear and great hope. Some would say we are witnessing the death of civilization as we know it, that we are in the midst of the great eclipse of Christianity. Others would say (and we would agree with them) that the human race (and Christians in particular) are on the edge of a great adventure, that we are at last on the brink of a global vision of *one* human race, a vision that has always been at the heart of the Gospel. The fourfold pattern challenges us to wider and deeper relationships. We can either risk the adventure or shrink from these exploding and expanding horizons, and retreat into an inner fearfulness and anxiety. "What can it all mean?" we ask ourselves. That awesome question of meaning can fill us either with foreboding or with hope. "What can I possibly mean?" is another question. However we phrase the great questions of life, we inevitably look for someone or something to help us find answers.

Saints and Heroes

The image of the spiritual life as a journey is ancient and universal. There are many before us who have undertaken this adventure. Saints and heroes of all faiths bear witness to the glories and the dangers, the heights and the depths, of such adventures. The poet Dante found himself led in spirit to the depths of hell and to the heights of heaven to bask in the love that made the sun and all the stars. When we read about the spiritual adventures of men and women in other ages, their descriptions often sound crazed, as if they were, for a moment, mentally thrown off their balance. That's why we need maps, guides, and treasures. We need these resources when we face the inadequacy of our own efforts, the awful poverty of conventional wisdom.

We have the example and wisdom of all those who have gone before us (that great crowd of witnesses). We are always in their company. They provide us with some of the maps for our journey. They warn us about the dangers and the pitfalls. They describe for us the glories and the joys.

We have the opportunity of forming spiritual friendships with all sorts of people on the way. There are pastors and teachers, confessors, and friends. There are those who may serve as spiritual fathers or mothers to us. Others act as midwives of the Spirit, helping in our rebirth, either dramatically or in some small way. We cannot develop and grow in the Christian life without such relationships. It is unwise to undertake the journey inwards without a guide, without a community of friends, without the support of an ongoing life. We should not plunge irresponsibly into the human adventure. We need the support of an ongoing life-bearing community, the body of Christ, the church. We are always in the company of the Saints who have made the journey before us. While our experiences will never be quite the same as theirs, nevertheless, there are dangers and glories common to all. We can profit from the records of our fellow pilgrims, stored in the treasure-house of Christian history.

A guide, whether one from the past or one alive and present with us now, can rescue us from our own narrow point of view. He or she can rescue us from the tyranny of the present where we imagine that the way we see things now is the only true vision. If he knows his job, a guide can cause a great upheaval within us to promote our continued growth. Those who are called to be guides often make disturbing connections. They tell us, for example, that there is a connection between our despair and loneliness and the love and providence of God. We find this both annoying and puzzling. They forge unexpected links between bread and wine and political and social realities, between the earth and those who live on it, between those who live in remote countrysides of the Republic of China and those who live in suburban Atlanta. It often takes a genius to make us see these inherent connections. Without the guide, the saint, the artist, we do not readily see the bonds of the Covenant that bind us to God, to the world, to others, and to our deepest selves. Jesus was the one who saw the freedom of the great

Covenant and made others see. That is why he was killed. That is why seeing and making others see can be dangerous. Jesus not only saw the relationships inherent in the Covenant, he was also its revitalizing power. He still is.

Types of Spirituality

Most people like to classify and label. It is more fun to watch butterflies hovering over a mud puddle or taking nectar from their favorite flowers—if you know something about their history, the kind of eggs they lay, their mating and migrating habits, and what they like to eat. We want to be able to name them. In the same way it is helpful and suggestive to know something about the different modes of spirituality. We learn to recognize ourselves by entering into the experience of others. When we speak of spiritualities in the plural we sometimes make distinctions based on historical periods, or we use the categories of theology, psychology, or sociology. We can speak, for instance, about monastic spirituality, the pietism of the seventeenth century, or the spirituality of the inner light as practiced by the Society of Friends (Quakers). Analysis deepens and sharpens our awareness of the infinite variety of the ways of God with humans. It helps to keep us from assuming unconsciously that our own way of living the Christian life, our familiar patterns of prayer, fasting, and almsgiving, are the only ones, or the *right* ones, or the best ones.

We should bear in mind, however, that the usefulness of dividing spirituality up into types is limited. First of all, there can be only one Christian spirituality. Human beings are made in one image, the image of God, and have one perfection, the perfection of love. There is one covenant relationship with God and with each other. Our relationship with God is that of daughters and sons of a loving Lord. Our relationship with each other is as brothers and sisters sharing the same mercy and making it real for others. We know that there are two great commandments of the Christian life: love God and love your neighbor. And we know that the duties of the Christian life are summed up in the Sermon on the Mount as prayer, fasting, and almsgiving. There is one promise of the coming Kingdom, one faith, and one poverty, one common human need for salvation, for ultimate security.

Remember not the sins of my youth, or my transgressions;
according to thy steadfast love remember me, for thy
goodness' sake O Lord!

Good and upright is the Lord, therefore he instructs
sinners in the way.
He leads the humble in what is right, and teaches the
humble his way (Ps. 25:7–9,RSV).

Second, each individual is unique, and classifications are true only in a general sense. All sorts of combinations are possible. Christian spirituality is a harmonizing of all our life under one transcendent value, the love of Christ. It cannot be defined, analyzed, or classified, because its meaning is not found on a level or reality where definitions are made. Uniqueness roots us concretely in time and space, history and geography. We share the mark of uniqueness with the simple things of the earth: the marvelous patterns carved in the wings of a butterfly, the outline of a fish scale, the spiral design of a pinecone or a fern, the geometrical diagram of a snowflake. Never are two alike. Uniqueness is one pole of our human meaning. Transcendence is the other pole. It keeps us from finding our ultimate meaning in the realms of the created order, whether physical, intellectual, or emotional. What we look like can be typed: short and fat, square, tall and thin—and so forth. How we think can be typed: logical or illogical, intuitive, imaginative, abstract, or concrete. We can also make categories to describe how we feel: depressed or elated, angry or sad or merry. Our degree of maturity, or development, can also be estimated. We are more or less conscious, more or less aware of inner realities, more or less socialized, turned inward or outward, and so on. But Christian spirituality in its essence cannot be classified.

With these limitations in mind, we turn to some of the

ways in which it has been described. First, we will consider some historical categories.

The Traditional Threefold Way

One of the most ancient divisions is that between the three classes of Christians: beginners, *proficients* (those who have made some progress and acquired some maturity in Christian discipleship), and the perfect (those who are established in the love of God)—in short, the saints. Along with these three classes, there is the conception of the three ways. These are commonly described as:

- **The purgative way,** that state or aspect of the Christian life in which the chief task is the routing out of sin and bad habits;
- **The illuminative way,** in which the chief activity is growth in virtue and in the knowledge of divine things;
- **The unitive way,** which is characterized by the stability of our communion with God.

It is easy to see that the three ways correspond roughly to the three stages of the Christian life. We owe this scheme to the theologians of the first five centuries of Christianity, and we recognize in it the influence of Greek thought with its tendency to divide the body from the spirit, to think of the good life as an achievement, and the ultimate goal as the contemplation of God. This way of describing our relationship with God corresponds to something in our experience and has its value, but it is a limited value. We have to see the whole process also in the light of our membership in the people of God, the body of Christ, the church, and reckon also with the Jewish and Christian understanding of body and soul as interrelated aspects of the human person.

The Three Elements of Religion

Another threefold distinction corresponds to some extent to the ancient one we have just described. It is that of the Roman Catholic lay theologian of the beginning of this century, Friedrich von Hügel, in his study of St. Catherine of Genoa, *The Mystical Element of Religion*. He describes religion as having three basic strands. The first is the historical, institutional, traditional strand. This is the aspect of spirituality into which we all come as babies. Our first religious experience is objective and corporate. Children learn to pray by sharing in the prayer of the family and the parish church. They do what they see others do. As they grow older they appropriate more and more of the tradition that is their heritage and that the church, through its ordained ministry as well as through the witness of its prophets and teachers of all ages and both sexes, preserves and guards as our common treasure.

The second element is the intellectual, the scientific, and the analytical. Here is the sphere of theology and philosophy, an area we begin to enter as we approach puberty and experience ourselves as individuals. There comes a time in the life of every boy and girl when the need for independence, for thinking it out for oneself, becomes more important even than the need for belonging. Most youngsters go through a period of doubt, commonly acted out in some form of nonconformity with family standards and practices. When this occurs in the area of religion, the child may be beginning a new phase of development, and not just experimenting with a new and more grown-up form of rebellion. It is part of the maturing of every individual to develop his or her own philosophy of life and to make some effort to confront basic issues, the mysteries of life and death, good and evil, freedom and destiny.

The third strand von Hügel calls *the mystical element*. By this he means the sphere of Christian life in which our personal relationship to God becomes conscious and important in itself. After the individual has entered the Christian fellowship, learned its ways, been nourished by its strength and wisdom, and has also done some independent thinking about these realities, the third element can begin to emerge.

The three elements are not like a series of progressive steps, grade one, grade two, and grade three, for instance. Being promoted to grade four means leaving grade three forever (although, of course, one does not leave behind all one learned from grade three). The three ways can be compared, not to successive stages, but rather to the ratlines on a ship, those rope ladders up which the seamen aboard sailing vessels used to swarm towards the top of the rigging. Ratlines are parallel. The sailor uses now one, and now another, as is handy. In the same fashion, both the three ways and the three elements are always there and can be used when they are needed.

Von Hügel further says that Christianity itself in the first centuries was chiefly institutional and corporate. He sees St. Peter as a symbol of this first element. The second stage, of course, was not wanting from earliest times. St. Paul is an obvious example, as St. John is of the third, mystical element. It is also possible to combine in one personality two or all three of the elements: St. Augustine, for example, combined the last two, and Cardinal Newman all three. Conflict between individuals often reflects the tension between two of the emphases, for instance, between thinkers and mystics, or between scholars and charismatics, or between people of the institution, the ecclesiastical hierarchy, and people of prophetic vision.

Sometimes representatives of the three elements or types can come together to enrich one another rather than fighting among themselves. A few decades ago, three of the members of the Anglican Order of the Holy Cross, who were stationed together in a West African mission, enjoyed many lively evenings together precisely because they were different. Each one represented strongly one of the three elements. The first man loved history and liturgy. He could remember rubrics, he learned all he could of the history and folklore of the people among whom he worked, and he had many practical and administrative skills. The second man was a scholar, interested in theology and language analysis. He was able to work out a comparison between two of the African languages spoken on the mission, and he was good at preparing catechetical material. The third man was a mystic. One day when he was just completing a visit to an outstation, a distant place that he knew he would probably never see again, an African came up to him and asked him, "teach me to pray." The advice he gave the man was, "I'm so sorry that I can't stay here long enough to teach you how to pray. But I can't leave without telling you this: go out into the bush by yourself and say to God out loud, 'teach me how to pray.' I am sure God will not refuse." The three men were friends, and their differences served to enhance their relationship and give greater efficacy to their work as missionaries.

Another classification is that between the once-born and the twice-born, made by the philosopher and psychologist William James. He saw the once-born person as the natural optimist, and called him "healthy-minded," in contrast to the twice-born person who is aware of and sometimes oppressed by the imperfections and sinfulness in himself and in others. James saw the second person as sick, but he also recognized that those religions that contain a pessimistic element are the most complete.

A final method of classifying the types of spirituality comes from sociology and is developed on the basis of *church type* versus *sect type*. In the first type, religious practice is dominated more by the institutional and historical, and in the second more by the prophetic and emotional. A third type is called *spiritualistic* and represents the unstructured worship of many *Free Churches*, charismatic, or Quaker groups.

All of these ways of categorizing religious experience and spirituality have arisen within the tradition of the Christian West, and they are useful when they are limited to that experience. They do not help much when we are confronted with Christians of the independent churches of Africa, native Americans who are beginning to develop an indigenous form of Christianity, or with the churches of the Far East. Just as it is important for us to expand our sense of responsibility for stewardship from the consideration of the needs of our own region or nation outwards towards an awareness of the overriding need for world justice, so we need to become aware of forms of spirituality other than our own.

The Witness of Africa

The African church, for instance, has given us its martyrs, its prophets, and its wise men. Those who have worked with African Christians are struck by some of the differences between us. For one thing, the African world view is a religious one in itself. There is no distinction between sacred and secular or between body and soul. All things and all people are held together in one by God who gives balance and harmony to all. Another fact that strikes many missionaries in Africa is the power to heal, both physically and spiritually, which resides in many African men and women, and which is also exercised through the ecstatic worship, singing, dancing, and fasting of the independent churches.

Yet another difference that strikes the Western observer is the capacity of many African Christians for spending long hours in silent prayer. For example, when the wife of one of the teachers in a Liberian mission school was having open heart surgery in the United States, her husband spent the entire day in the church in prayer, without eating or resting, and this seemed quite usual to the other African Christians. It was the white missionaries who thought it remarkable.

The Spiritual Guide

Do you have a *friend of the soul*? It may be someone very close to you who would be shocked if you described him or her as a special spiritual friend. A healing presence is simply there. This kind of friend is rare, but a great joy when the gift comes.

Sometimes we're given a special friendship for only a short time, perhaps only an hour or even a few minutes. All that is needed is a word of healing or of judgment that cuts so deep within us that we feel the surge of new life. Others of us have the privilege of enjoying long-lasting friendships that have nurtured and sustained us over a long period of time.

From time to time it is good to enter into a special relationship with a spiritual director who can help us more systematically and formally to grow in Christian commitment. This is a person we can see or write to on a regular basis; someone we can trust; someone whose stern as well as encouraging word we respect. Spiritual directors are hard to find.

There is, however, one kind of spiritual guide available to us all. This is an inner guide who is nothing less than the Holy Spirit. We have to be careful not to get our voice confused with his. That's why we've said over and over again that Bible reading, regular sharing in the Eucharist, and belonging actively to the Christian fellowship are vitally important for a properly balanced spiritual life.

It is also possible to enter into a positive and imaginative relationship with a guide from the past; with, for example, the great figures of the Old Testament. We can use our imagination when reading the New Testament. Jesus comes alive to us in the Bible. Abraham, Moses, Peter, and Paul become, in meditation, our contemporaries. So do St. Augustine, Martin Luther, John Donne, and St. Teresa—and a host of others.

There are many traditions, many maps, and many guides. We have wonderful resources at our disposal. The question is, are we willing to ask for help? Are we willing to listen? Are we willing to receive from the hand of others?

· 20 ·

The History
of Christian Spirituality

We now return to our own tradition and consider a few of the most significant historical types of spirituality. We have seen that there is basically one Christian spirituality. The first disciples shared in the life of prayer, fasting, and almsgiving of the Jewish church of their day. A specifically Christian form of prayer and interpretation of fasting and almsgiving gradually emerged within the gatherings of the first Jewish Christians. The early church that Luke describes in the Acts of the Apostles met, we are told, for prayer and the breaking of bread, sharing and handing on the Apostles' teaching. They held possessions in common. This pattern of spirituality was their interpretation of the call to discipleship.

During the age of martyrdom in the first three centuries, a new spirituality was formed within the Christian community through the terrible pressure of persecution. The literature of the church of this age, such as the letters of two of the great martyrs, Ignatius and Polycarp, and the writings of Origen, seem to breathe a spirit of light and serenity that is surprising. They see Christ everywhere: in the bishop, in the deacons, in the confessors, those arrested and imprisoned but not yet executed, as well as in the martyrs themselves. Their duty of *doing kindnesses*, as the Jews sometimes described almsgiving, was accomplished by carrying the sacrament to those imprisoned. Christians exhorted one another to withstand the torture, and served one another at daily peril to life and limb.

When the Edict of Constantine (313 A.D.) delivered the church from persecution and established it, first as a legitimate and then as the official state church, the spirit of the martyrs found a new form in the monastic life. It was the early monks and hermits who sought to carry out what they saw as the highest form of Christian witness in the sacrifices of an ascetic life. The conflict was no longer with beasts in an arena but with the demons of the desert who tempted men and women to forsake the difficult way they had embraced.

The early fathers and mothers of the desert responded to the call of Christ literally, as it is expressed in the Gospel of St. Matthew: "If you would be perfect, go, sell what you possess and give to the poor, and you will have treasure in heaven; and come, follow me" (Mt. 19:21). Leaving all that they had, they went out to live in solitary places where they might be alone with God. Their form of ministry consisted in hospitality to strangers and, after they had undergone a long training in the ascetical life, in the giving of spiritual direction to those who came to them. There were two basic forms of the monastic life, that of the solitaries or hermits, and the life of those who lived in community. The latter stressed corporate worship and works of mercy, while the hermit life always emphasized solitary prayer and manual labor. Very early in monastic history a form of spirituality that interpreted Scripture in the light of Greek philosophy indelibly marked the monastic life. The Greek tendency to divide human beings into body and soul, and to assign the passions to the body and regard them almost as intrinsically evil, influenced these Christians in their understanding of the whole of the Gospel. In particular, they understood that part of it that requires us to sell all, to deny ourselves, and to take up the cross if we are to follow Jesus as involving the renunciations of marriage, possessions, and all worldly pursuits. Monasticism has produced an enormous body of spiritual theology in which a negative attitude towards the body and the society of the world is implicit. For centuries, indeed, until the Renaissance, except for sermons and catechetical material, there was no other Christian spirituality to speak of available to Christians in or out of the monasteries. During the Middle Ages, some of the great religious orders developed lay groups called tertiaries. These men and women wanted help and guidance in living the Christian life where they were, in families, in towns and cities, living as artisans, farmers, housewives, traders, and merchants. The rules that governed the tertiaries were adaptations of the monastic rules. Secular spirituality did not yet exist.

The situation of Heloise, a famous learned woman of the twelfth century, is an example. She was a pupil of Peter Abelard, a great teacher and philosopher, then his mistress, and finally his wife. It was unheard of for a scholar in those days to marry, even if he were not a priest, and the marriage was in trouble from the beginning. Heloise's uncle, infuriated by Abelard's behavior, plotted against him and sent a band of men to overpower him in his room one night and castrate him. Eventually he found refuge in a monastic life, and he seems to have been able to accept monastic spirituality for himself, but when he put Heloise into a convent, and after her profession set her as abbess over the community of women that he founded, she was not able to accept a monastic way of life as her own. She complied outwardly, but she cried out inwardly, and to Abelard in private. She protested that she was not able to live this life for God. She objected to the rule she had been given and begged Abelard, her lover and her husband, as well as one of the greatest scholars of Europe, to give her some guidance about how she could live a Christian life when in her heart she was a wife and not a nun. Abelard had nothing to give her except the same monastic rule, and with this she had to make do.

The Reformation

It was not until the Reformation had exploded within Christendom and knocked apart the three strands of spirituality— the institutional, the intellectual, and the mystical—that the humanism of the Renaissance began to unfold, and new forms of spiritual life appeared. In the churches of the Reformation the traditional liturgical and sacramental worship was displaced by a new kind of service in which preaching and extempore praying were central. The emphasis upon justification by faith and the understanding of faith as a personal saving gift, touching one's heart and will, transformed the sermon into one chief means of grace. The reformers reacted strongly against what they called a *religion of works*, outward things one could do to gain merit and earn heaven. Much of the paraphernalia of medieval devotion was swept away, the good with the bad. Out went most saints, relics, crucifixes, missals, copes and miters, incense and holy water, confession and the mass. And out from the monasteries and nunneries, in a small but increasing trickle, went many religious, leaving their houses and renouncing their vows. Luther, of course, was one of these, and as is well known, he married a former nun. Devout family life began to take the place of the monastic ideal within the reformed churches, and the new humanism, which expressed itself with such expansive power through all the orders of society, gave expression, through music and literature as well as in sermons, to a new spirituality.

The three elements of religion tended to break apart under the twin pressures of reformed doctrine and secularism. New orthodoxies and new ecclesiastical institutions were produced in the form of national churches; new rationalizations of dogma appeared, leading eventually to Deism in the eighteenth century (that high and dry doctrine of God as the divine watchmaker whose Presence is not required for the smooth running of the universe. He is the absentee God who lives "out there."). It is not accidental that Methodism came to birth in such a dry period. The love and fervor of the first Methodists warmed many a human spirit who had thought that God was absent from his creation. There were other movements too, which rose up in reaction to Deism. For example, new pietist groups began in Germany, centered on deep personal devotion to the Redeemer, but with little theological or institutional structure.

The Anglican Way

At its best, it shows spiritual good manners, a quality no less valuable in the religious life than in social life, though, of course, not the ultimate criterion in either, reverence without religiosity, and humor (in which last trait it resembles Jewish piety). Like all styles of piety it becomes detestable when the fire of love has gone out. It is no insult to say that Anglicanism is the Christianity of a gentleman, but we know what a tiny hairsbreadth there is between a gentleman and a genteel snob. [1]

The quotation above is from W. H. Auden, and his point is a good one. There is something peculiarly English about Anglicanism. It has its bad side in its tendency to arrogance, but it has its good side in openness, generosity, and gentleness. The fervor of the Reformation was tempered by the English character. Indeed, the English Reformation differed from that on the Continent in many ways and for many reasons. One can trace in the parties within Anglicanism the same splitting up of the three elements of religion. The High Church party emphasized the traditional and historical, the Broad Church was marked by rationalism, and the Evangelical party, with its stress upon individual conversion, represented the mystical element. However, all three of these elements coexisted in the Church of England. Harold Browne, Bishop of Winchester, addressed his diocesan conference in 1889 on the vexed question of party division in the Church of England. He used Charles Simeon, John Keble, and F. D. Maurice as examples of generous Anglican comprehensiveness. He had known all three men personally. Bishop Browne stated:

I could heartily subscribe to the chief tenet of Simeon's school, that Christ is the only way to salvation, and that no creature, earthly or heavenly, can intervene between the soul of the sinner and his Saviour. I can subscribe to Keble's faith in the assured presence of Christ in His Sacraments, the communion of the individual with his Saviour, and the indwelling of the Holy Spirit, and the Communion of Saints. And I can join heartily in the teaching of Maurice that the Eternal Father regards with all-embracing love those whom he has created and redeemed.

The coexistence of the low, the high, and the broad elements were seen by Bishop Browne to be part of the generosity of Anglicanism.

One way of describing this coexistence is to point to the *via media* (the middle way) as common to all three. It was a convergence strong enough to hold them together in an uneasy tension. The first Anglican theologians, men like Richard Hooker and Jeremy Taylor, were men of the middle way, a spiritual location between Rome and Geneva. Their center of reference, theologically, devotionally, and to some extent liturgically, was the undivided church, the church of the Fathers of the first ten centuries of Christianity. The Anglican appeal to authority established by these men and others was threefold, and appealed to Scripture, to the tradition of the early Church, including the first four General Councils, and to the intellect and conscience of each individual under the guidance of the Holy Spirit. The task of the Christian believer, then and now, is to discern the will of God through the interaction of these three courts of authority.

The *via media* preserved within Anglicanism a wide range of traditional spirituality, both Protestant and Catholic. Many traditionally Catholic and Protestant insights were filtered through the English temperament and reshaped by the peculiarities of the English language. It is not accidental that Anglican spirituality has been nurtured by two seventeenth-century masterpieces: the King James Version of the Bible (1611) and the Book of Common Prayer (1662).

English spirituality laid hold on the richness and variety of the new forms of literature, music, and art that were developing with such profusion and distinctive beauty in English culture, beginning with the age of Elizabeth. The piety of the Caroline Divines (those theologians who lived about the time of the reign of Charles I), the new monasticism that took shape in the family of Nicholas Ferrar at "Little Gidding," and the poetry of George Herbert and John Donne represent a new flowering of English spirituality. The *via media* can also be mediocre and colorless, a perhaps overly safe and sane compromise with the world.

Over and over again in history, when the Christian church becomes too closely identified with secular power and the surrounding culture, the Holy Spirit seems to raise up within her women and men of protest. Sometimes they are fanatically one-sided personalites. They may be uncouth, illiterate, or violent. Some of them are mad. Nevertheless, they may speak for God. Jacques Maritain points out in *Theonas: Conversations with a Sage* that there are some effects of the justice of God that it would seem he would have at all costs. If he cannot find someone to bring them in mercy, he will raise up others in revolt to bring them in ruins. The Reformation was such a revolt, but the *via media* tradition in England prevented it from being as explosive and divisive as it was on the Continent. England did not entirely escape a war of religion, though the Civil War (1642–1649) was less destructive than those religious wars that raged for so many years across the Channel. The pieces were picked up again with the restoration of a Stuart king, Charles II, in 1660, and the established Church of England resumed her stately ways.

Her spirituality had been enriched by the new humanism, and she developed a whole literature of spiritual direction, teaching her children holy living and holy dying in the ordinary world of labor, commerce, and the state, as well as in the home. In the middle of the nineteenth century, monasticism was revived in the English church and made its contribution by strengthening and enriching the life of public worship and private contemplation and prayer. Religious houses offered hospitality to guests, spiritual direction to those who sought it, and the opportunity for retreat. The Evangelical revival to which John Henry Newman owed his conversion and the Oxford Movement, which he and Pusey, among others, launched and directed, roused the established church from lethargy, gave it new energy and depth, and provided a theological foundation for a more fervent Christian life. Men like F. D. Maurice and Archbishop Temple awakened her slumbering social conscience. The ancient duties of prayer, fasting, and almsgiving were given fresh embodiment within the English church.

Two world wars later, we find ourselves in a new situation. As Anglican Christians we bring the treasures of our inheritance with us as we face the future. The world seems more deeply divided than ever, between the affluent, technically developed West and the poverty of the Third World, and between the Marxist and capitalist ideals of the good society. The divisions between the Christian churches mean less and less, especially to young people today. There is a great thirst to be one in Christ and one in the Eucharist, but there is less interest than there was a generation or so ago in the patient work of theological definition and the construction of new and more comprehensive ecclesiastical and theological structures. It is easier to leap over the wall, and many do it. By sharing in the devotion and faith of other groups, we deepen and enrich our own. We also tend to relativize our own positions. Most of us no longer feel it is appropriate to pray that Baptists, Roman Catholics, and Presbyterians be converted to the Episcopal Church. We hope instead for a wider and truer vision of the one church to be given to us as we grow in love and compassion for one another across denominational lines.

The Emergence
of a Contemporary Spirituality

God is on the side of the oppressed. Our world, through science and medicine and democratic reforms, has abolished many ancient forms of oppression, yet we are dismayed at how many new tyrannies and new poverties divide and threaten human solidarity. The Holy Spirit has raised up in the church in our day as in every other day new forms of worship, discipline, and service. New liturgies express the old faith and devotion in new ways, including within their scope the concerns and hopes and fears of the contemporary world. They show a new awareness, for example, that creation is fragile and precious, and they pray that we may learn to serve it with reverence and restraint.

Religious orders are turning from preoccupation with institutional work and have discovered new forms of contemplative life and witness to the most suffering of our brothers and sisters. The Little Brothers and Sisters of Jesus, the brothers of Taizé, the sisters of Grandchamp, and many others like them are carrying out a ministry of presence and friendship with the poor. They have gone into the violent and poverty-stricken places of the world, to live there simply, earning their own living as others do and maintaining their houses as small centers of prayer where others may come freely to share their worship and friendship. God is giving us new models not only for prayer and devotion, but also for fasting and almsgiving, for self-discipline, simplicity of life, and the doing of kindnesses. Not all of us are called to the quiet heroism of the Little Brothers and Sisters of Jesus. Nevertheless, each one of us is called to be a unique and irreplaceable presence in the world. Individuals and even institutions have been renewed and healed by the simple ministry of a prayerful presence. This is the great work any Christian can undertake.

Glimpses of Anglican Spirituality Today

Instead of trying to analyze the spirituality of American Christians, Anglicans, or American Episcopalians according to historical types of any of the above schemes, we shall try, finally, to describe some of the types of spirituality that can be encountered in the world in which we live today. We shall begin with the life of an Episcopal seminary in a large American city, and then move outward from the school to the city itself and beyond.

In the seminary, the most obvious expression of spirituality is the daily worship of the chapel, where Morning Prayer, the Eucharist, and Evening Prayer are offered according to the Book of Common Prayer. Evensong is generally rendered solemnly. The faculty arrays itself in academic dress, with tippets and hoods, and enters in procession, and students sit in the stalls or outside the rood screen with guests. The office is sung, and, on feast days the officiant wears a cope and censes the altar at the Magnificat.

On Tuesday nights the pattern changes. There is a family
Eucharist with a sermon. Families often sit together, and the
faculty stalls are sometimes invaded by faculty children. A
few babies come, and some of them cry. The service is sung,
and the hymns are usually more familiar ones. In addition to
the formal worship of chapel, there are a number of informal
worshiping groups within the seminary. Some meet for
shared Bible study, intercession, and song. Guitar music,
prophecy, interpretation, and mutual concern expressed in
prayer may characterize these meetings. Another group
meets for silent prayer together, based on the theses of the
church year. Spirituality at the seminary is expressed
officially through the liturgical year with its feasts and fasts,
and through occasional short retreats. Unofficially there are
many other expressions: a silent vigil of prayer in protest, a
protest perhaps for which words could not be found; an early
morning hour of prayer and Bible reading; another kind of
vigil, at noon, during a fast day for world hunger.

What we have described is typical of Anglican spirituality,
with its emphasis upon the objective corporate tradition of
liturgical worship. At its center is the Eucharist, the principal
act of Christian worship, and together with the daily offices,
the firm and stable element in our life of prayer. At its worst,
it degenerates into formalism. At its best, it is the central
source of life, for the parish or the institution, flowing out
strongly beyond the boundaries to the world beyond. It is
interesting that the two types of prayer groups that have
appeared at the seminary spontaneously are groups that offer
complementary emphases to institutional worship: quiet,
contemplative reflection on the one hand, and a more lively
and personal expression of individual faith, joy, sorrow, and
concern on the other. Both are expressions of the mystical
element of religion.

The third Christian duty is called *almsgiving*, and covers
our service to those in need. The form which almsgiving
takes at the seminary is first the familiar collection plate, the
proceeds of which go sometimes to the seminary chapel
itself, for bread and wine, for candles and soap, brushes and
brooms, which are needed to keep the physical edifice going,

and sometimes for special causes, such as the Presiding Bishop's Fund for World Relief, or the churches in Africa. There is a committee for Mission and Social Action that sponsors programs directed to the relief of local needs and sometimes to consciousness-raising with regard to particular issues: world hunger, disarmament, and the liberation of the oppressed.

Leaving the seminary and going out into the wider experience of the diocese, we visit one of the parish churches in the inner city. It is a well-established church in a racially mixed area, with a long record of active and effective social involvement. Its worship is traditional, somewhat in the old Anglo-Catholic style. The Eucharist is the central service, celebrated in Spanish and English. The daily offices are recited, and the special seasons of the church year are celebrated not only with music and incense, but also with bright banners made by a parish group. The music that is sung is also a product of the worship experience of the congregation. It was written by a composer who is also a parishioner and whose work is grounded in parish participation. The kind of prayer group that, among others, has arisen in this parish takes a different form from the two at the seminary. Its members meet together to reflect quietly upon the appointed readings for the coming Sunday and to share these reflections with one another. The emphasis is partly upon sharing with others the way in which Scripture speaks to each one about our common Christian discipleship.

It is not difficult to see how the three elements of religion, the institutional, the intellectual, and the mystical, are represented in this sketchy account of some forms of worship in the Episcopal church in an urban setting. The institutional and traditional are strongly represented in the public worship in the seminary and the parish. The intellectual element is emphasized in the seminary by preaching and in the parish also by the prayer group, while the mystical element is given expression at the seminary especially in the Quiet Days and in prayer groups. We must remember that these are only examples, and many more pictures could be painted depicting the various ways in which Episcopalians worship.

The Breaking Down of Barriers

A hundred years ago the barriers between churches were high and thick. Each one cultivated its own garden, and each felt superior to the other. The climate is very different today. It is now possible to see the various elements represented by the various traditions as having a legitimate place in the worship in the one great church. Church unity as an ideal is no longer described in terms of uniformity, but rather of a wide sharing of treasures. The worship forms and habits of different Christian groups are a precious part of our inheritance.

We can take a wider view yet of worship by looking at the Navajo reservation. The chapel of one Navajo mission has been built of red-purple stone from the local mountains, and its woodwork is painted turquoise blue. The metal work has the silver color of aluminum, which, with the blue of the paint, recalls the colors of traditional Navajo jewelry. Within, the stone gives a warm feeling to the whole building. There is a central stone altar and the sanctuary floor is covered with Navajo rugs. Holy Communion is distributed clockwise, because this is the traditional greeting order in a Navajo hogan. Both English and Navajo are used in the service, and there is a great deal of lay participation by men and women, and girls and boys, who serve as acolytes, interpreters, and members of the choir. Two objectives dominate the life of the missions: learning how to incorporate and express a native American spirituality in a Christian congregation, and empowering the Navajo people to take over leadership at every level. There is now a Navajo priest, and decisions are made by the mission councils. The remaining white missionaries are colleagues and fellow Christians, not bosses.

We have tried to trace some of the complicated relationships between many types of Christian spirituality. We have tried to see our spiritual heritage from the perspective of history and to analyze it from the point of view of sociology and psychology. Christian spirituality has its own inner consistency. In all of its manifestations, it reveals one unifying work of the Holy Spirit within creation, from its deepest center to the tiniest and most outward finishing detail, constantly transforming it into a beautiful whole for the praise and glory of the Father.

We have also seen that the spirituality of every age uses the forms—social, artistic, literary—of the surrounding culture in which to express itself. Every spirituality is relative. There is no one right way to pray, to celebrate the Eucharist, to fast, or to do good. As we try to find our own way in the world today, we make use of models from the past and from other cultures, but we also offer to God our own new, little creations. We pray in words that arise from our own deepest consciousness, our own experience, and we try to incarnate the vision of discipleship for today.

· 21 ·

Living Prayer

The whole object of Christian discipline in prayer is the transformation of human life by the power of the Holy Spirit. "The purpose of living is not to learn to make prayer. It is to become prayer, to live in and for God." Our living life to the full *is* prayer. Prayer is the transfiguring of all our being and doing. It is as if there is within each one of us a wounded or maimed yet lovely person waiting to be healed and restored. An arm or a leg has been broken, and the glorious but crippled human being within needs nursing, nurture, and exercise if he or she is to be vigorous and healthy again. When we begin to exercise, all our faculties—our desires, longings, our memory, imagination, and will—the life of God himself begins to flow in our veins.

Prayer is one of the means by which harmony and balance is restored so that the image within us comes to life; the sick person inside us is healed. There is an interior revolution by which the human spirit becomes again what it truly is, the work of the Holy Spirit. Or again, there is something like a chemical reaction whereby a dead thing is brought back through the energies of a life-giving Spirit.

It is true that we cannot make healing happen, but we can, on a disciplined daily basis, make ourselves available to God in prayer. This availability to God in prayer can be unsettling and even devastating. It is nothing less than the remaking of our very being. Prayer is an act of self-surrender that often feels like death. New life comes to us only when we allow the old self to die. That is why we may speak of Christian prayer as a taste of death and resurrection. It is the Spirit of God moving over our chaos, brooding over our darkness, and calling us always to himself, always to new life. In prayer we make ourselves available to God, who is constantly available to us, so that we can experience our own genesis, our own coming into being.

Prayer Is Availability to God for the Inner Events of the Spirit

In a sense, all the mighty acts of God that we find recorded in Scripture have to happen to us. In the book of Genesis the Holy Spirit broods over the chaos at the first creation. So, too, the Spirit broods and hovers over our chaotic life. All the great events of the life of Jesus are also inner events for every Christian. Many of the saints remind us that it is little use for us to celebrate the birth of Christ in Bethlehem 2,000 years ago unless Christ be born in us. We have to open ourselves up to a Bethlehem within. So, too, with the Crucifixion, Resurrection, and Ascension. To be *in Christ*, to be shaped by him, is to die with him, to be raised by him, and to ascend with him to the right hand of the Father. These are the inner mighty acts of God in prayer, which continually call us beyond what we know of ourselves.

> In the beginning of creation, when God made heaven and earth, the earth was without form and void, with darkness over the face of the abyss, and a mighty wind that swept over the surface of the waters. God said, "Let there be light," and there was light . . . (Gen. 1:1–3, NEB).

Fiax lux! Let there be light, and there was light. Light is an important symbol of the loving and creative presence of God. In fact, the symbol was so powerful that many people thought of God as literally light. Light is still a very powerful symbol for the nurturing and pervasive presence of God. It not only suggests the lighting up of dark places in the physical world, but also the illumination of the dark places of mind and heart. It can also describe both our expanding awareness of things and the awakening of a sensitive and compassionate conscience.

Light is a symbol of the all-embracing presence of the God we call *Immanuel*. He dwells among his people. That is to say, the Biblical understanding of the way things are is focused in God's continuing and enlightening presence, in the various patterns of relationship in the idea of covenant. This is the basis for all our praying. Our prayers do not *make* our relationship with God. They celebrate it. They encourage us to live in it. They remind us that God has given himself to us completely and utterly in Christ.

Prayer: The Celebration of an Alliance

Christians recognize and acclaim God as Immanuel: God bound up with his people. Christian prayer expresses this bond. We believe that human life is patterned on this fundamental fact, and our very existence relies on a complex pattern of lesser covenants, common allegiances, agreed-on conventions. Life is a cooperative enterprise or it is nothing. Prayer becomes in Christ a cooperative communal activity that celebrates this great Covenant that God has with us and with the whole of creation.

From the point of view of the Bible, prayer is inconceivable as a separate *religious* activity. Prayer is, in effect, the celebration of the alliance. We shed tears of joy and of sorrow; joy because the bond is sure, sorrow because of our failure to see and live truly within the Covenant. For the Christian, then, there is no aspect of human life that is not the concern of this basic fundamental Covenant relationship with the living God. There is, therefore, a great deal of what we might call *unconscious* or unrecognized Christian prayer. It is reticent and self-effacing like the Spirit of God himself. It is expressed in small things done unselfconsciously. In tiny gestures, in a still, unassuming presence, in the sharing of a meal, in the trust of a friend, one finds the heartbeat of prayer.

Prayer Is Being Available to God

So the life of prayer consists in the various ways we make ourselves available to God. It requires definite acts of listening, of waiting, of opening ourselves up. Our God does not force himself upon us, although He is always closer to us than we'll ever know. This amazing reticence and deference of God is supremely expressed in the Incarnation, in his totally identifying with everything that we are, in submission and lowliness, putting himself at our mercy.

> Let your bearing towards one another arise out of your life in Christ Jesus. For the divine nature was his from the first; yet he did not think to snatch at equality with God, but made himself nothing, assuming the nature of a slave. Bearing the human likeness, revealed in human shape, he humbled himself, and in obedience accepted even death—death on a cross. Therefore God raised him to the heights and bestowed on him the name above all names, that at the name of Jesus every knee should bow—in heaven, on earth, and in the depths—and every tongue confess, "Jesus Christ is Lord," to the glory of God the Father (Phil. 2:5–11, NEB).

Our availability to God, to the world, to one another, and to our inner selves is really what is meant by the life of prayer. It is life in its totality, rooted and grounded in this basic relationship. Trust in this relationship is beautifully described in the Letter to the Ephesians:

> With this in mind, then, I kneel in prayer to the Father, from whom every family in heaven and on earth takes its name, that out of the treasures of his glory he may grant you strength and power through his Spirit in your inner being, that through faith Christ may dwell in your hearts in love. With deep roots and firm foundations, may you be strong to grasp, with all God's people, what is the breadth and length and height and depth of the love of Christ, and to know it, though it is beyond knowledge. So may you attain to fullness of being, the fullness of God himself (Eph. 3:14–19, NEB).

Here is the life of prayer described in a nutshell: to be so available to God that we become that which mysteriously contains the uncontainable. Our destiny is to share in the life of God himself. If it is my destiny, then it is yours and the destiny of every human being. Our destiny in God, once it has been seen and believed, affects all our relationships: to the world he has made, to our fellow human beings, to ourselves. We are both individually and collectively the temple of the Holy Spirit. "Do you not know that your body is a shrine of the indwelling Holy Spirit, and the Spirit is God's gift to you?" (1 Cor. 6:19, NEB).

Prayer, then, is the development of the art of communion. We are called upon in our own generation to develop the disciplines required for loving and open communion with God, the world, others, and ourselves. We need to recover the art of communion and so recover the universe as God's, and rediscover our roots in God, in the world, in one another, and in our inner selves.

Prayer: The Celebration
of God's Gracious Availability to Us

Christian prayer, then, is the total expression of a life, a life surrendered in love to God, the Blessed Trinity. The contemplation (seeing) of God in the things he does and in the things he has made pushes us into action, into mission, and thrusts us all into pilgrimage. Christianity is not a way of passivity. Although it is true that there is a great deal of waiting in Christianity, this quiet waiting for God becomes the source of great energy for working in the world.

The Christian life of prayer, or the Christian life prayed, is a supremely human way. The way to God is through our humanity, our joys and aspirations, and also our disappointments. Our medieval mystic put these words into the mouth of Christ:

> No one can attain to divine heights or to unusual sweetness, unless he be first drawn through the example of my human bitterness. The higher one climbs without passing through my humanity, the deeper one falls. My humanity is the way by which one must go, my sufferings are the gate through which one must go, my sufferings are the gate through which one must pass, if one would attain what thou seekest.[1]

We should never forget how ordinary prayer is, how commonplace. The God whom we seek is not far from us. He is in our flesh. His presence is in our bones. He suffers in our suffering. It is in our hearts that the Spirit of God is to be found.

The human heart is, according to the Christian tradition, *a capacity for God*. It is *God-shaped*, and the pattern of our relationship with God is through an intimacy with the world he has made and through our relationships with one another. We long for both meaning and intimacy, but often we do not know what we want. Many would deny that their inner hunger is a hunger for God at all. But to avoid the use of the word *God* we have to use tortuous circumlocutions. Theologians have struggled with phrases like *ultimate concern* and *ground of being;* atheists with *the dialectic of history* and *the will of the collective;* Americans with *our manifest destiny* and *the American way of life.*

Thomas Traherne, writing in the seventeenth century, spoke eloquently about our hunger for God:

We love we know not what: and therefore everything allures us. As iron at a Distance is drawn by the lodestone there being some Invisible ways of conveyance by which some great Thing doth touch our soul and by which we tend to it. Do you not feel yourself drawn with the Expectation and Desire of some Great Thing?[2]

This "Great Thing" for a Christian is focused in and identified with Jesus Christ. His Spirit is the invisible communication between God and humanity. He was a human being like us, a knowable yet unfathomable mystery like ourselves. The pattern of our living is to be seen in the saving rhythm of the life of God himself. St. Augustine described God as always active, always at rest. His life is peace and action. Our life is "struggle *and* contemplation," to use the phrase of Frère Roger Shutz, the Prior of Taizé. Our life in God is engagement in this life, here and now.

"If I lack a sign, I seek no other but this," wrote John Donne, "that God was made man for me. And that God and man are so met is a sign to me, that God and I shall never be parted."[3] Our aim, our goal, our end as human beings is to be centered in that relationship with God in a communion of love. St. Thomas Aquinas put it this way: "The final end and happiness of the human being is essentially the vision of God."[4] To be human is to *see* God and then to become like him, to imitate what we *see*. Thus, the Christian spiritual tradition affirms that the desire to see God and to be like him makes up our very being and is the sign of who we are. To fail to see and to live by what we see is to have failed at everything. So, true happiness without God is inconceivable, since a human being is, by definition, a movement towards God.

> Let us bless God who has given us being, and a being which has a relationship and a movement towards him. That movement is impressed by the Creator's power in the depths of his creature, deep within it from the very moment of its creation. And it is a movement so deep and so powerful that the will cannot affect it except to fight against it, that no sin we commit can hold it back, that hell itself cannot obliterate it.[5]

Christian prayer rests on this wonderful assertion that a fundamental relationship exists between the Creator and his human creatures. Unlike some other spiritualities, Christian spirituality is not concerned with an experience of some kind of impersonal reality, but with a relationship of communion with that personal reality that we call God.

We may sum up our conclusions about prayer as follows:

- Christian prayer is based on the grace of God, and communion with him is sheer gift and not dependent on skills or techniques.
- Such disciplines can only create an environment in which the Spirit can freely work and are always subordinate to the demands of love.
- There are dangers in the journey inwards, and there is a need for guidance and help along the way.
- Christian spirituality is concerned with the whole of reality: with the ugly as well as with the beautiful, with tears as well as with joy, with evil as well as with glory.
- The heart of Christian prayer is in worship, particularly

in the Eucharist, where we share sacramentally in the drama of salvation.

- The focus of Christian prayer is the Scriptures, the book of the acts of God. It is in the act of *remembrance* in word and sacrament that we are put in touch with our true selves, and because of this we may live in hope.
- In the end, there is no war between prayer and action since Christian prayer, rooted in God's giving himself to us in Jesus Christ, is the highest form of action. Christian prayer is committed to the art of making connections, of forging creative relationships. There is an intimate link between an interior life in Christ and the mission of the Church and the world. There is, therefore, nothing outside the concern of Christian spirituality. Political and social questions are of the utmost importance to the praying Christian.

Using Brother Ass

St. Francis mockingly and lovingly referred to the body as "Brother Ass." The body is enormously important in prayer. Not only is our posture important but the actual condition of our body. Our inability to care for the body by eating too little or too much, by neglecting its well-being, naturally affects our prayer life.

The position of our bodies often shows our state of mind. In fact, many books have been written on body language, because we know that the body *speaks*. I wonder what the crouched and tortured body positions of our prayer signify?

In prayer our bodies should be relaxed, but not so relaxed that we'll fall asleep. Our minds should be collected but not forced by concentration. When we are praying, we are to have that focused and still attention of the bird watcher.

There are many books available today on techniques of prayer and the use of the body in meditation. *Living Simply through the Day* by Tilden Edwards is one such book.

Make yourself comfortable. Breathe deeply, and close your eyes. Do not pray, but allow yourself quietly and simply to become prayer.

Part Four

THE CHRISTIAN IN THE WORLD

· 22 ·

Building the Human Community

Prayer is an encounter with the Creator–Spirit who made and sustains, loves and approves, the works of his hands. Every Eucharist is a mystery of the mingling of flesh and spirit. The Christian tradition is rooted in the unified view of reality found in the Old Testament. We know that worship and prayer are not purely spiritual, for we are not pure spirits. They have their bodily expression in song and dance and in fasting and watching. The codes of law found in Scripture make no distinction between spiritual and material regulations, and the prophets denounced two great sins equally: apostasy, the worship of other gods; and the oppression of the poor.

Jesus' own life shows an alternation of days busy with work, teaching, and healing, and nights of silent communion with the Father, alone in a quiet desert place (Mk. 1:35). Immediately after the scene on the mountain of the Transfiguration when Jesus enters the cloud of glory and the contemplation of the Father, he descends the mountain and comes face to face with a man possessed by a demon. He passes immediately from deep communion with the One God, in ineffable light, to a very troubling experience, a meeting with a mad man from the region of meaninglessness and darkness.

The prayer of Jesus is not always in solitude. It springs from his profound immersion in the world, in temptation, in suffering, and in the human joy of being used for the healing of a friend. Jesus prayed in Gethsemane, on the cross, and at the raising of Lazarus.

From the days of Isaiah of Jerusalem to our own, prophetic voices have warned us that we cannot separate prayer from action.

> even though you make many
> > prayers,
> I will not listen;
> your hands are full of blood.
> Wash yourselves; make yourselves
> > clean;
> > remove the evil of your doings
> > from before my eyes;
> cease to do evil,
> > learn to do good;
> seek justice,
> > correct oppression;
> defend the fatherless,
> > plead for the widow (Is. 1:15b–17).

"You cannot worship Jesus in the sacrament of the altar and sweat him in the bodies of his poor," said Bishop Frank Weston, missionary Bishop of Zanzibar, preaching to the Anglo-Catholic Congress in London in 1923.

Michael Ramsey, the former Archbishop of Canterbury, put it this way:

The Church of Christ has a like journey in Christ's name, towards heaven in adoration and into the heart of the world in serving it. While the two facets are really one, there are in our present imperfection those moments which are primarily worship, in silence or in word, and those moments which are primarily the service of humanity, in energetic actions. [1]

Concern for the poor and oppressed is part of every Christian vocation as it was part of the duty of the people of

God from the beginning when they entered into a covenant relationship with him. The earliest of Israel's law codes gives a basic motivation for mercy towards the weak and the disadvantaged:

> You shall not oppress a stranger . . . for you were strangers in the land of Egypt (Ex. 23:9).

The stranger, like the widow and orphan in tribal society, is grouped with the poor. The motivation implied in "for you were strangers" is unique in ancient codes and enshrines a precious principle: we ought to give to the poor not because they are worthy, but because we share in their basic condition, a condition of need. We, too, are entirely dependent upon God, who meets our every need whether we are worthy or not, and we are to imitate his universal benevolence, showering benefits alike on the just and the unjust. Unless we do recognize our poverty, we cannot turn to God in true prayer, lest he say to us, "You are so full of very self, there is no room for me." We know that Christ is in the poor and the persecuted, upon whom he looks with special love, and we can always find him there. The great parable of the last judgment tells us that it is by our response to human need that we shall be judged. "Truly I say to you as you did it to one of the least of these my brethren, you did it to me" (Mt. 25:40).

We Hand on to Others What We Have Received

The relationship between prayer and action is expressed in the Dominican motto: to hand on to others what one has received in prayer. The Dominicans were founded as friars with a vocation to preaching and teaching. They were called to give others the fruit of their contemplation and study. The kind of action that Christian discipleship involves differs from age to age and from person to person. At the center of all discipleship is the call to sell all, give to the poor, take up the cross, and follow Jesus. For the rich young ruler selling all and giving to the poor meant just that—literally. The church in Jerusalem carried out its call to discipleship through the sharing of their possessions, so that nobody in the fellowship lacked for anything. Later, during the terrible years of persecution, material possessions were of small importance. What the Christians had to share was rather mutual encouragement in persevering under torture, constant prayer and intercession for the *confessors*, as those were called who suffered for their faith, and carrying the sacrament of the Body and Blood of Christ to those in prison. Those who ministered to their fellow Christians in this way shared the most precious things they had and did so at the risk of their own lives. This was their interpretation and expression of selling all, giving to the poor, and taking up the cross.

After the days of persecution were over, a new form of Christian action emerged within monasticism. Some of these, for example, the monasteries of women and of men in Asia Minor, under the direction of St. Macrina and St. Basil, engaged in works of mercy, the care of children, the rescue of the starving, and the maintenance of hostels for the aged and hospitals for the sick. From that day to this, Christian institutions have ministered to many kinds of human need in all parts of the world.

From the earliest days of the church almost until our own day, the duty of liberating the oppressed and ministering to the afflicted has been thought of in terms of the rescue of needy individuals. This was the first form of the *works of mercy* and is an abiding one. These are the poor who are "always with us," disadvantaged members of our own family, associates, personal friends, and personal enemies, under our noses and in need, and we can and must "do them good."

There is, however, another aspect of our duty towards others that has been emerging more clearly in our own time, and that is the social aspect. For millennia, for Jews and Christians alike, poverty was understood in terms of what the sociologists now call *case* (or individual) *poverty*. The works of mercy were meant to relieve the needs of unfortunate individuals. No one until modern times seems to have recognized that class (or group) poverty is due to social and political causes that can be remedied by cultural, economic, and political means. The existence of large classes of poor and oppressed people, including slaves and serfs, was taken for granted almost everywhere in the ancient and medieval worlds. There is nothing in the Bible to suggest that the poor should be helped by more just laws, higher wages, or better working conditions. It is not even suggested that slavery as an institution was wrong and should be eliminated. The concept of *class poverty*, created by a self-perpetuating and dehumanizing system, is a modern discovery. New sociological insights into the causes of human suffering have begun to evoke new forms of Christian action, against the torture of prisoners, for instance, for *human rights* generally, against the destruction of the grazing lands needed by Native Americans to preserve their way of life in particular, and towards the control of the arms race and the elimination of chemical, biological, and nuclear warfare.

Christians have begun to see that the hunger that exists today on such a vast scale cannot be eliminated by an increase in personal giving, for instance, although that is a necessary first step, as a stopgap measure. The sad fact is that if our giving is limited to sending food to the hungry, however generously we respond, we are not only failing to meet the need, but we may be making matters worse in the long run. The guidelines for enlightened, organized Christian giving have been revised to shift emphasis from relief and rehabilitation to programs that foster the development of local resources and basic education. Self-giving on a different level from that of direct sending of food is required by such a revised program.

As with world hunger, so it is with other pressing issues: the oppression of racial and cultural minorities, in our own as well as in other countries, the widening gap between the affluent and the destitute, and the waste and pollution inherent in an economic and industrial system that depends for its functioning upon endless expansion of production and hence upon the using up of irreplaceable natural resources.

Christian Prayer
Penetrates and Changes Things

If Christians are to see their mission in terms of penetrating and converting the structures of the world, we shall need new symbols. The separation of church and state is a deeply rooted principle in the United States, and religion is not supposed to interfere with business, politics, or the ordinary institutions of daily life. In a pluralistic and secular society, indeed, it should not. We need, however, a symbol for our sense of relatedness to the social whole, and our mission regarding it. The Fall took place in a garden, but it is a city that stands for the consummation and redemption of all creation. "The holy city, new Jerusalem, coming down out of heaven from God, prepared as a bride adorned for her husband" (Rev. 21:2). The Kingdom of heaven is not only seen as a city, but it is described as *inherited* (Mt. 25:34). It is given to the poor in spirit. Discerning the place and time of this giving is part of the singular vocation of contemporary Christians. So is the discovery by each of us of our own expression of poverty of spirit. A new form of ministry is emerging in the secular context, where Christians are called to be the salt of the earth, as "poor yet making many rich."

Another new form of Christian ministry has arisen from the monastic orders. In the place of institutions organized for the work of teaching and converting others, some groups have expressed their discipleship through their ministry of presence. Instead of trying to teach others better ways of doing things, a procedure that implies superiority on the teaching end and inferiority on the receiving end, groups of brothers and sisters become friends with the poor and oppressed and share their lot. They live in some of the poorest parts of the earth, by the work of their hands, and their ministry consists in solidarity and in friendship. In this way tiny cells of Christians have entered the slums of Bangladesh and the *bidonvilles* of Algiers. They have gone out to find Christ in the poor, to contemplate and love him there. Their fellowship with exploited people gives them an opportunity to receive their own spiritual riches from the poor and to give in return from their own.

Contemplation leads to action. The same Holy Spirit who teaches us to pray also teaches us what we are to do with our gifts and where our limits are. We are limited, and the needs of the world are oceanic. If we try to do everything, we end up by doing nothing. One aspect of the discernment of spirits has to do with matching up our limitations and primary commitments with our availability. The Spirit helps us to decide whether we have the time, the strength, the empathy, and the ability to respond to specific persons and causes. The call to discipleship, to Christian action, is a corporate one, and each of us seeks to find his and her own place in the healing and reconciling mission of the Christian community.

Community and Communities

Politically and socially, it is becoming more and more important for our survival that we view the world and the human race as one. This basic unity that is now being pressed upon us by necessity has always been an important part of the Christian vision of reality.

No vision of the Christian God is complete without a vision of a redeemed and recreated human community. How is this community built up? This book began with the birth of a baby. There is the basic human community: the coming together of a man and woman, and the birth of a child. The very first community to which we belong is our family. Sometimes it is a repressive community, but it is, for good or ill, the place where we first became persons. As we grow up, that small community widens to include the local community and the nation. We begin to move out of the narrow confines of family and from other ties and allegiances. We may work for a giant corporation or a large institution. Christians, too, move from the family into the parish, which itself is part of a diocese, which is related through the office of the bishop to the whole world. Of course we don't cease to belong to a family or to a parish when we grow up and begin to have a sense of the oneness of the whole world. It's just that these smaller communities we now see as an expression of that one community which God has made: the whole human race.

INTENTIONAL COMMUNITIES

Christian community is built up through various kinds of small groups within the larger unit. The healthy functioning and growth of a mission, a diocese, a parish, or an institution such as a school, a seminary, a hospital, depends upon the soundness of the relationships within the subsidiary groups. Jesus called his disciples "that they might be with him," and through the interaction of the disciples among themselves and with their first leader they were prepared for their mission. At Pentecost, the little group, enlarged by the presence of Mary the mother of Jesus, was transformed, endowed with new power, and turned outwards towards others, first to Jews and then to Gentiles. In this original group we find the genes of the church. The characteristic marks of a Christian community passed on from generation to generation and took on different expression from age to age, but the Spirit working deep within it kept the basic organic structures of being true to form.

These smaller groups that formed within the church, families, extended households, local churches, dioceses, guilds, and later monastic communities and many other institutional forms, constituted the Body of Christ. Since they carry the genes of this body of which they are living parts, the smaller units also live by the Spirit, bear witness to the resurrection of Jesus, and are open to those outside. They meet for prayer and worship, for the Eucharist, and for common meals, and they share what they have, first among themselves and then to meet the needs of those without.

In our own day, new forms of community have multipled. The older monastic orders still exist in their varied forms, and in some places are vigorous, although many of the active religious communities, especially, have been declining in membership since the 1960s. Other forms of residential communities have appeared, some of them including married people who wish to live a common life of prayer and work and to dedicate themselves to a common task.

Still another form of community is that called *intentional*. An intentional community is a group of people that shares some aspects of a fully residential community such as a monastic order or a commune, but without sharing living quarters or accepting total community of goods. The general purpose of an intentional community is to give mutual support in the development of Christian vocation. Some intentional communities are, for example, focused upon agriculture, some upon social work, and some upon ecology. Others concentrate upon the personal and spiritual building up of their members for various forms of service. The members accept a common rule of life, which they adapt to fit their particular needs and which includes the provision of time together for worship, reflection upon Scripture, discussion of common interests, and a common meal. Some of these groups are loosely organized from a common center, such as the Community of the Cross of Nails, centered upon Coventry Cathedral in England. Others are more closely related to such monastic communities as Taizé in France. The rules of life that these groups have developed and that form the basic discipline for each member include provisions for the regular practice of silence and meditation each day, an ordered plan of study, participation in the corporate worship of the church, service to the community or the poor, and a regular pattern of self-discipline. This latter may include guidelines about health, rest, food and drink, recreation, fasting, the control of income and expenditure in order to give to others, and the sharing of burdens.

One of the exercises of an intentional community that is in use in some contemporary religious communities such as Taizé and Grandchamp is called *révision de vie*. It is a difficult phrase to translate, and perhaps a description of the exercise will be the best way to show its function as group spiritual direction.

Révision de vie is the sharing, in a small group called a *foyer*, of one's experiences as one engages in Christian pilgrimage. The purpose of this sharing is to help the members grow in the knowledge and love of their fellow Christians in the group, to test the authenticity of their sense of vocation and direction, and to receive from and give to others by sharing the insights and challenges that become clear as the members explore their own spiritual experience. The larger communities of Taizé and Grandchamp are divided into several *foyers*, forming small personal centers within the life of the whole, and they can be helpful in suggesting patterns for other kinds of Christian community.

Each *foyer* has its own meeting place, and its membership is relatively stable. The usual size is about seven or eight persons. The meeting for *révision de vie*, which takes place each week, is prepared for by personal prayer and study that focuses on the Eucharistic readings for the coming Sunday, or upon specified parts of the Rule, or the notes from a recent community retreat. In this way all the small groups are considering the same theme at the same time. The meetings begin with the reading aloud of the passage agreed upon. This is followed first by a period for silent reflection, which may last for five or ten minutes, and then by an informal sharing of each person's insights or reaction to the reading. These groups are not study groups, and hence intellectual analysis and elaboration are out of place, although what each one says will be formed by whatever work or study has gone into the preparation. Dialogue and debate are not encouraged. Each person is to be free to say what struck her in the reading and how it challenges, stimulates, or judges her own life. For the most part, the other members of the group listen quietly, considering and savoring what is said, and refrain from efforts to correct or confute one another. There may be some gentle questioning in order to draw out more of the meaning, but there is no argumentation.

Another thing that these groups avoid is the use of techniques of therapy. There is no conscious effort made to deal with others' feelings, to confront or to probe, to comfort, or to modify behavior. The group has not come together for therapy or for problem-solving. Members may bring problems, temptations, or spiritual and emotional crises to the group, but they do so in order to show where they are, in order to be better known in the Spirit, and to inform others of their need for intercession and thanksgiving. They do not expect the group to provide solutions.

One of the fruits of this kind of discussion is a deepening of respect and love for the other members of the group, each in his or her uniqueness before God, including the uniqueness of each one's suffering; another fruit is the gradual creation of a strong bond of love that binds together persons of very different temperament, taste, and ability, as well as different ages. This bond is not based upon natural attraction or compatibility, but upon the common union of Christians in the Lord. It fosters loyalty, concern, and affection among the members without cutting them off from other *foyers* or from the community as a whole. The structure of the *foyer* is balanced by the comprehensive structure of the larger community in its meetings for worship, meals, work, and discussion.

Révision de vie fittingly closes with some kind of common meal, informal recreation, and conversation. About two hours a week are spent in this way at Grandchamp.

There are many adaptations of the general pattern of intentional community. There is nothing to prevent a *foyer* from engaging in other types of meetings, and some are essential, for instance, a regular discussion of practical and business affairs, planning, and the conscious orientation of the group and every member in it toward the larger community. The quality of community life depends upon the health and vigor of the relationships within it. Keeping the *foyers* open to each other and to the central administration in mutual frankness and affirmation, and the encouragement of the members in other kinds of association are essential if they are to avoid the elitism and the formation of in-groups which threaten every Christian community.

· 23 ·

The Art of Christian Presence

Contemplation is "seeing the world aright," and as such, clears the mind for action. Contemplation is the means by which we accept the fact that we are creatures, that we are finite. This fresh way of looking at things is an important antidote to self-importance, to our so easily getting puffed up. Contemplative prayer (simply being present to God and to one another) prevents our getting blown up out of proportion. It is strange how we behave as if we are gods, as if we really are going to live forever. A sense of our creatureliness is related to that healthy if misunderstood virtue called humility. It is facing the facts. When we face these facts we can then get on with the business of living. This realism is expressed in the great service of Morning Prayer (the Daily Office), which is one of the main beams that holds together the fragile fabric of the Church. In the *Venite* (Ps. 95) we say every day:

> O come, let us worship and fall down
>   and kneel before the Lord our Maker
> For he is the Lord our God,
>   and we are the people of his pasture,
>   and the sheep of his hand.

And again in the *Jubilate* (Ps. 100):

> Be ye sure that the Lord he is God;
> it is he that hath made us and not we ourselves;
> we are his people and the sheep of his pasture.

Things Really Do Change
in the Light of Christian Presence

Christian prayer rests in the givenness of God, his *isness*. It may seem painfully obvious, but say it we must: **God is!** Our primary experience of him is the same as that of Moses described in Exodus 3:

> Now Moses kept the flock of Jethro his father in law, the priest of Midian: and he led the flock to the backside of the desert, and came to the mountain of God, even to Horeb. And the angel of the Lord appeared unto him in a flame of fire out of the midst of a bush: and he looked, and behold, the bush burned with fire, and the bush was not consumed. And Moses said, I will now turn aside, and see this great sight, why the bush is not burnt. And when the Lord saw that he turned aside to see, God called unto him out of the midst of the bush, and said, Moses, Moses. And he said, Here am I. And he said, Draw not nigh hither: put off thy shoes from off thy feet, for the place whereon thou standest is holy ground. And Moses said unto God, Behold, when I come unto the children of Israel, and shall say unto them, The God of your fathers hath sent me unto you; and they shall say to me, What is his name? What shall I say unto them? And God said to Moses, I AM THAT I AM: and he said Thus shalt thou say unto the children of Israel, I AM hath sent me unto you (Ex. 3:1–5, 13–14, *KJV*).

When Moses turned aside to see the great sight of the burning bush he began a course of *action* which was to change his whole life and the lives of his people. His simple act of contemplation was the prelude to that great Biblical adventure we call the Exodus. We, too, are invited to *turn aside* and sit in humble worship before the awesome and wonderful reality we call God. Intellectually, it means we are asking the question behind all questions: "Why is there anything at all and not just nothing?" Spiritually, it is seeing into the mystery of things and responding with a song of praise. We echo God's word in creation ever returning to himself in the joy and power of the Spirit. This is what we mean when we say that Christian prayer is rooted in the life of the Holy Spirit and undivided Trinity.

When we *turn aside* to be still, to contemplate, things begin to happen, things quite outside our control. The world begins to change for us and for others in the light of that which we have contemplated. When we meditate on the life of Christ as portrayed in the Gospels, when we allow those stories and events to penetrate our consciousness, life begins to change, because after the act of God's giving of himself to us in Christ, human beings were never quite the same again. God has chosen us to be the signs of his presence in the world. Christians in their living and in their praying are called to be what all human beings are called to be: sacraments, signs to and for one another, of God's indwelling presence in his world.

The special way of being present to God and to one another is difficult to describe. It is the powerfully focused presence of two lovers. We know those times when we have been totally and imaginatively present to the person whom we love. But more often we are only partially present to one another, no matter how involved we may be. In our hearts we are far away, absent from the people who are actually sitting in the same room. The kind of presence we ought to have in Christian living is like the quiet stillness and close attention of a sensitive artist who would photograph rare and nervous animals.

Being present in this way to other human beings requires that we pay close attention to them as mysteries, as the lively images of God. This loving presence to our brothers and sisters, to the whole of Creation, is what is actually required of every Christian. It is a sharing in the compassionate and loving gaze with which God regards the world he has made. Compassion is at the heart of this quiet, prayerful, and loving presence.

The Art of Compassionate Presence

Compassion is also at the heart of conviviality, of our living together. To live with and in God, in his world, with his people and with oneself, involves compassion. Compassion is the ability to enter imaginatively into the lives of others, and to feel joy and pain with them.

If my brother or my sister is a lout, a delinquent, a snivelling failure, then so am I. If he is touched with glory, given to visions, capable of heroism, then so am I. When we are truly present to one another we begin to see that there is one race, one destiny, that there is solidarity in sin and solidarity in glory. We belong to one another in wonderful intimacy. We are what our brothers and sisters are, because, as we have seen, we are made of the same stuff and stamped with the same image and likeness. To be compassionately present to our fellow human beings is the way into our understanding of what intercessory prayer is. To pray for someone to be so totally present to someone that, just for a moment, we *become* that person, and by the miracle of compassion we begin to learn what it really means to bear one another's burdens.

To catch a glimpse of that intimacy, that solidarity, means that we can never be the same again. To be present to one another means a deep joy and a deep pain shared in a common life. We are all joined together in our flesh and blood. There is a common flame burning in the heart of every person. It is the light shining in every human being (Jn. 1:9). We are, at all costs, to pay attention to that light, to tend and guard that flame.

The Ministry of Quiet Presence

The ministry of quiet presence allows others (perhaps wounded or nervous) to approach the fire, bask in its heat, and be flooded with its light. We in our turn are warmed and illumined by the quiet accepting presence of others. How are we to cultivate this except through silence, stillness, prayer?

To do this we have to give up our desire to be either inferior or superior to others. We have to embrace an alarming doctrine of genuine equality. That is not the naive understanding of the equality of the cookie-mold. We are not all the same in that sense; we are not pressed out on a production line. There is, however, an equality of presence, an equality of love, an equality of our being children of one Father. Each one of us is loved uniquely for our individual self, but each one of us is bathed in an equal light. When we begin to understand that kind of equality, then the glorious differences between persons begin to emerge. There is, indeed, one human race, but what variety, what color, what gifts! In being present to God and to one another we can then enter into another person's pain or joy at a level where it can be shared. It is an exhilarating and fearful experience. This is not an easy camaraderie. It is the creative presence of a person who is content to wait and quietly enter the pain and the joy of another. There, we share the strange intimacy of our condition. We know that we are mortal. We know that we share a common destiny. It is there that we can begin to minister to one another.

Christians, committed as they are to the life of prayer, to the adventure of interior exploration, are those who are called to be compassionately present to their brothers and sisters. The art of contemplating another person as mystery means that we can really see a brother or sister in the meanest and lowliest of persons. It means that we can really see in them something both beautiful and wonderful. But it does not mean our embracing a sentimental view of our fellow human beings. Christian compassion is active—it springs out of a contemplative attitude which seeks to understand the true nature of things and people.

Christian spirituality is concerned with a common vision of meaning which we Christians proclaim and celebrate as a community of presence. It is to the specific content of our fourfold vision that we must eventually turn. How does a spirituality of compassionate presence work itself out, first in our own being, centered in Christ, and then in our relationship to God, to the world, and to others?

We Are to be Present to the World in the Same Way that God Is Present to Us

We have seen that the desert of Sinai was the place of pilgrimage between Egypt and the Promised Land. In that desert an unformed, ill-disciplined rabble was forged into the people of God, into a people whose God actually lived in their midst. These strange people, with Jehovah in their blood, were to be a sign to the nations of the Presence of this One God. This presence shows itself in the frailty of human flesh, in the ordinary events of human life. Christians affirm that God and the human race are so met in Jesus Christ that the two will never be parted. We are, God help us, to be signs of the divine presence in the world. What kind of presence is it? What kind of God is present in the life, crucifixion, and resurrection of Jesus Christ? What does it mean to be present in and to the world in the way God himself is present? It means following the path of the Exodus. It means a desert experience. It means following Jesus as the Spirit drove him into the wilderness to be tested (Lk. 4:1–13).

Christian realism demands that we do not evade the hard but freeing questions that the desert poses: questions concerning evil, sin, and darkness; questions concerning acts of inhumanity, greed, and exploitation. Our prayer life as Christians will involve a daily Sinai experience, a daily carving-out of a desert place in our hearts, a daily waiting for the Presence.

This waiting on the Divine Presence in the desert of the human heart is ninety percent of what Christian prayer is: as we have seen, it takes on different forms. Sometimes it is a peaceful and centering experience; at other times it is a bursting out of joy and praise. Sometimes we are frightened and cry out in sorrow; at other times we simply wait. The desert is a rich place of prayer, but not always a comfortable one. The saints believed that this daily desert experience freed them to enjoy the world all the more. It was a bare place, austere and wild. We might, in exasperation, cry out to them: "Open your eyes! Look at the glories of creation!" They would reply: "When I go to my desert place and close my eyes I catch a glimpse of the glory of the One who made them all. It is then that I can really enjoy them. There is no fear of loss since everything belongs to God."

The Presence of God in the Desert

We are able then, little by little, to see the Presence of God in all things without falling into the trap of imagining that the created order is God. The great temptation is to fill that emptiness, that desert place, with the presence of thoughts, feelings, things that crowd out the holy presence of God. We get impatient with waiting. It seems too much like laziness and passivity to many of us. We can hardly believe it's the preparation for creative and energetic activity. Yet this is what the desert experience signifies: a *preparation* for action. The *first* act of the ministry of Jesus was to be driven by the Spirit into the wilderness. After that he was able to set his face towards Jerusalem.

There is, in the desert experience, both a sense of panic and a sense of promise. There is the promise of new life, new possibilities. There is the panic that nothing will ever happen in all this emptiness and stillness. It all seems such nonsense, this waiting on the Holy Presence, and we cannot live for very long with nonsense. In our panic we set about furnishing the empty space. We are like a newly married couple setting up house. The truck is at the door and is quickly unloaded. The empty house soon becomes a nest, a home, a place in which to relax. Everything is in order. Things must have their proper place and be called by their proper names. Real freedom, we argue, depends on our understanding that there is a time and a place for everything. But the desert experience tells us that the times are out of joint. There is a hole in the world and all the light seems to be running out of it. In our panic we try to plug the hole with anything that comes to hand: a worn-out ideology, an old fashioned heresy in a new suit, a spirituality forged out of the bits and pieces of broken therapies and half-believed religions.

The Costliness of Presence

Christian Presence (if it is to be Christian) faces the emptiness, the void, the bankruptcy at the heart of human life. The quality of our presence in the world will depend precisely on what we do with the great gaping hole in the heart of things. It is in the *desert place* that we face the worst and the best life has to offer. We face our darkest selves, we wait for the light of God's Presence. We will have to face nothing in this life more terrifying than ourselves, nothing more pregnant with hope and with possibility than the recreative presence of the Holy Spirit. We must enter the wilderness with Christ. We must follow the example of the children of Israel and leave our *Egypt* and journey into the desert so that we may enter the Promised Land. What does our particular *Egypt* look like? Our *Egypt*, like the one described in the book of Exodus, is a place of contrasts. To be sure, it is a place of slavery, but it is also a place which we call home. The Israelites, when they were in the wilderness, remembered their place of enslavement with longing. The manna which God gave them to eat in the wilderness was nothing in comparison to the rich and varied diet of their slavery:

> O that we had meat to eat! We remember the fish we ate in Egypt for nothing, the cucumbers, the melons, the leeks, the onions and the garlic; but now our strength is dried up and there is nothing at all but this manna to look at (Num. 11:4–6).

The slavery of power, money, or sensuality seems preferable to the wild freedom of the desert. And why not? We want to conserve all we can, with every ounce of our power. Common sense, we argue, demands that we act out of self-interest. Some will have to suffer. I hope I won't have to. Some will have to die. I hope it's not my turn just yet. But that's life. You take all you can and hope for the best. This hoping for the best isn't that easy for those of us who are trying to live in a violent society. We live in an age of economic and social instability. We live on a planet plagued by the specter of terrorism, of mindless and gratuitous acts of violence against one another and against the earth, the seas, and the air, not only in distant lands but close to home. We say our prayers, go to church, and hope for the best. The Christian Gospel demands much more of us than this. We are called to be signs of the Presence to this world now.

Christian Presence will mean standing out in direct contradiction to the values which reduced parts of the world to a
state of terror and which threaten social and economic
stability everywhere. Christians will have to be the pioneers,
with others, of a different way of thinking, a changed style of
life. This is why the issue of spirituality is so important
today. We now know that we cannot simply go on as we
have been, expanding politically and economically. Many
people realize this and are anxious to develop ways of living
more simply and expanding inwardly our minds and hearts.

There are now virtually countless ways in which a human
being can embark on a program which purports to be one of
interior growth. It is big business. The issue is, of course,
one of faith and not of the development of techniques to
ward off despair. Creative presence in the world, to the
world, in the way God has revealed himself in Christ, is not
achieved by programs or committees. In fact, it is not
something we achieve at all. It comes as a gift of the Spirit as
we wait in the desert. It is the Spirit that turns our relationships upside down. He it is, who by speaking to us quietly
in the depths of our own hearts, reminds us that *Egypt* isn't
our real home after all. It is with him. Home for us is the
place where God dwells. It is not *here*, nor is it *there*. It is
where God is.

The New Testament insists that our citizenship, by which
is meant the focus of all our being and doing, is in heaven.
The word *Commonwealth* and the phrase *Manner of life* are
used to translate words from the same root (Phil. 1:27 and
3:20, and Eph. 2:12). The desert experience of waiting on the
Spirit is a reminder of where our home truly is.

The Sacrament of Holy Presence

The Sacrament of Holy Presence in the world doesn't require
the organization of a program of renewal; it requires a
waiting on God. It requires our doing nothing, not in order
that nothing may be done but in order that God may do
something in us. There is in the heart of humanity a clear
hunger for God which no program can ever fill. There is a

hunger for holiness, for healing, for wholeness. Christian renewal means a renewal of holiness rather than the development of organizational skills. Saints, men and women of genuine Holy Presence, were the ones who, in the power of the Spirit, were the agents of renewal in the past. We cannot expect to be called to anything less than to a life of holiness: to be so transparent to God that his light shines through us into the life of the world, and into its structures, organizations, and programs. It is a daunting and exciting vocation, but one which many are eager to embrace. We have spent years re-ordering our prayer book, arguing over ordination and liturgy and the appropriation of funds (all very important things in our common life). Now there is a need for us to confront the living God.

When we do face the reality of God in our lives, we begin to realize that we do not, after all, belong to ourselves. This realization brings us to our knees in repentance. Why? Because, no matter how much we think so, we do not live our own lives. Each person imagines that the sovereign and free self is an instrument of a power outside and beyond itself. The fact is, that as a free and conscious self, you can yield to more than one power. You are free to yield to powers other than the power of God. The Christian believes that his freedom lies in his surrender to God and to him alone. All else is slavery. The Christian lives and moves in the presence of him whose service is perfect freedom.

The empty space within will not be filled by anything less than the infinite God. It will not be filled by a church or even a religion. It will not be filled by a regime of dieting, a course in *transactional analysis,* or *transcendental meditation.* It will not be filled by reading this book or any other book, nor will our spiritual hunger be satisfied with a program of Zen meditation or with the reading of Tarot cards, or with organic gardening.

How do we begin? "After all," you may object, "I cannot suddenly start relating to God. I need something more modest. God is too big." Well, we can begin with the things he has made—with clouds and trees, with dogs and cats. You might start by taking a long look at that tree outside your window. If that's too difficult, begin with the tips of your fingers. See what it means to be a creature, to be a thing made. You are not something self-created or self-perpetuating.

People, however, are usually inept at the contemplation of detail. We are too busy. We are not good at developing patterns of intimacy, because that development requires a desert stillness. Our inability to develop intimacy with others, to listen to them, to share ourselves with them in all our vulnerability and nakedness, means that we are continually diminished and impoverished at our very center.

The ability to be present to others presupposes an awesome yet free-wheeling intimacy with God. Slowly we are being brought face to face with the God who waits for us in the center of our own emptiness, where a monster broods over the desert, and the light is running out of the hole in our world. God is waiting there.

Although the Christian way is the joyful and exhilarating exploration into God, it begins with our realistically facing the emptiness within. Only God can fill our emptiness—so we must wait. As Christians, we wait for the One who can bring creative order out of our chaos. Faith's name for that great One is Jesus Christ.

Jesus Christ is God's Word to us about ourselves. He is a word of love, and the life of prayer is our road back to love. It is not, in the end, a question of intelligence and technique. It is a question of love. Nothing else matters. The shape and content of that love is seen in the life, death, and resurrection of Jesus.

All prophets and pseudo-prophets claim to bear the Word of the Lord. They traffic in the Word and claim that theirs is somehow a final one. They want to tell us who we really are and what we ought to do. But only God knows who we really are. The secret of who we are is held safe in his Presence. We believe that Christ is calling us to be our true selves. He is calling us home. We need to listen. There are many voices calling. Which voice is real? Which is illusion? Prayer takes patience and a sensitive ear. It is not always easy to tell the difference between a word of life and a word of death. There is glory and danger in all spiritualities. Quietness, stillness, waiting are essential, because without them we are scarcely aware of what we are doing. Each new thing tends to call into being its opposite. An over-balanced grasping at the truth on behalf of one point of view tends to call forth its deadly counterpart. We will have to be careful for the balance and equilibrium of things. Christians are to be the guardians of the equilibrium. That can sound dull, middle-of-the-road, and mediocre. It is not necessarily so. We need a passionate moderation: passionate in its determination that no one have the last word. The last word of all comes only from the creative silence of God.

St. Augustine describes God as *semper agens—semper quietus:* always active (or acting), always at rest. Christian spirituality is centered in this godly equilibrium. The focus of Christian spirituality is the drama of liturgy, in which joy and tears are equally expressed. The Eucharist is the meeting place for all of us.

Transfiguring Presence

Christians, then, are meant by the grace of God to be a transfiguring presence in the world. Often we have to be content simply to be there, present in and to a situation. Christian spirituality as a way of love fosters an unpretentious yet permeating presence in the affairs and lives of men and women. One early Christian writer expressed this in a letter to his friend Diognetus:

> For the distinction between Christians and others, is neither in country nor language nor customs. For they do not dwell in cities in some place of their own, nor do they use any strange variety of dialect, nor practice an extraordinary kind of life. This teaching of theirs has not been discovered by the intellect or thought of busy people, nor are they the advocates of any human doctrine as some are. Yet while living in Greek and barbarian cities, according as each obtained his lot, and following the local customs, both in clothing and food and in the rest of life, they show forth the wonderful and confessedly strange character of the constitution of their own citizenship. They dwell in their own fatherlands, but as if sojourners in

them; they share all things as citizens, and suffer all things as strangers. Every foreign country is their fatherland and every fatherland is a foreign country. They marry as all people do, they bear children, but they do not expose their offspring. They offer free hospitality, but guard their purity. Their lot is cast "in the flesh," but they do not live "after the flesh." They pass their time upon the earth, but they have their citizenship in heaven. They obey the appointed laws, and they surpass the laws in their own lives. They love all and are persuected by all. They are unknown and they are condemned. They are put to death and they gain life. "They are poor and make many rich"; they lack all things and have all things in abundance. They are dishonoured, and are glorified in their dishonour, they are spoken evil of and are justified. "They are abused and give blessing," they are buffeted as evildoers, when they are buffeted they rejoice as those who receive life. . . . To put it shortly what the soul is in the body, that the Christians are in the world. The soul is spread through all members of the body, and Christians throughout the cities of the world.

The quiet contemplative stance of the creature simply waiting on the Creator helps to liberate *God* from our narrow and imprisoning possessiveness. We wait, and we begin to see. When we see, we are made aware of the truth of God's wonderful intimacy with the things He has made; we do not have to look very far for corroboration. It is in the center of every human life, in the ordinary and in the commonplace. It can be found in the small heroisms of duty and routine when we begin to understand that it really is "He that hath made us and not we ourselves."

As we have seen, we seem to be experiencing the breakdown of those creative relationships which have kept human beings together. We've lost touch with the sources of power. We feel like Moses. We catch a glimpse of the Promised Land, but are prevented from entering it. Unlike Moses, our vision is blurred. We sometimes feel powerless to make creative connections, to make an environment in which human beings can grow and develop happily together. What we seem to have lost is the art of conviviality, the art of living and loving together. We have, as it were, forgotten the Covenant in much the same way that the Children of Israel kept forgetting their Covenant with the Lord. The prophets were the ones who kept calling Israel back to their first love, to their fundamental allegiance. So too the life of prayer is a return, a continual turning to affirm that basic relationship we have to God.

· 24 ·

The Future Is God's

We have traveled far and wide in our exploration of what it means to be a human being. From the Christian point of view, being human involves simply two basic relationships. The first is our relationship with God (at which we have looked with regard to the mighty theme of *covenant* in the Old and New Testaments). The second is our relationship with one another. This double relationship patterns and shapes the whole of human life. There are two phrases from two great Christians which emphasize this double relationship. The first is from St. Irenaeus (c. 130–c. 200): "The life of man is the Vision of God and the glory of God is a human being fully alive." Human life is the vision of God. In fact human life to be and to remain human at all requires vision, insight, prayer. The second phrase comes from a monk of the Eastern Church who lived earlier in this century, the Staretz Silouan. He simply said: "My brother is my life!" Notice that devastatingly powerful little word *is*. The staretz didn't say "I must love my brother." He went further by claiming that there is a disturbing intimacy which exists between all human beings. Full human life is an intimate union between God and the whole human race. As we have seen, that union is focused and made personal in Jesus Christ. He is the one who binds us to God and to one another. "The life of man is the Vision of God!" "My brother is my life!". These two phrases sum up the life of prayer for us Christians. It is the vision of God that binds us all together and that the Christian seeks to keep alive in all his praying and doing.

Presence in the World

What then is our task in and for the world? What are we supposed to do? We are to be, in Christ, a creative and open presence in the world for its transformation and transfiguration; we do this in three ways: by listening; by responding; by imitating.

Christian Presence in the world requires a good ear, the ability to listen carefully, to pay close attention to what is given to us in every moment. Only when we listen can we properly respond to what God is asking us to do. We have seen that right action only comes after contemplation, after a serious act of listening, seeing. When we have the courage to listen and the insight to respond, then things begin to happen. We find that we can be agents of transfiguration and transformation far beyond our puny capacities and limited vision. God is able to use us insofar as we are willing to make ourselves available to him.

Leaven and Salt

Agents of change: we are surrounded with them. From palm leaf fans to a giant air conditioner, from the compounds that soften water or the stubble of your beard, to those that drive away your dog's fleas or relieve your aching back—all of these things and more are agents of change. Some work better than others.

Two of the symbols for change agents that occur in both the Old and New Testaments are salt and leaven. Both are humble things, used in everyday life. Their action is unobtrusive but of crucial importance in their effect upon the substance they enter. How can bread rise without yeast? Who wants cereal without salt? Not even the Lord: "You shall season all your cereal offerings with salt; you shall not let the salt of the covenant with your God be lacking from your cereal offering; with all your offerings you shall offer salt. (Lev. 2:13). Salt is a preservative and a symbol of community; to *share a man's salt* means to enter into a sacred covenant with him, a relationship of hospitality or friendship. Jesus said to his disciples, "You are the salt of the earth" (Mt. 5:13) and "Have salt in yourselves and be at peace wth each other" (Mk. 9:50). Christians as salt are to be in the world and not of it. As agents of change they are to be in daily, humble, and often unseen contact with the world without losing their individuality, their unique quality. Salt goes into almost every pot and brings out the flavor of almost every kind of food.

We make a large claim, however, when we say that Christians are *the salt of the earth.* When we look at the history, for instance, of the Western world, can we say that Christianity has made a difference? We can point to the abolition of the slave trade, for instance, but it took nearly 2,000 years of struggle. There is a great fortress-like building, one of several on the coast of Ghana, at a place called Elmina. It was built as a trading post and served as a place where the slaves captured in the interior were gathered together to be shipped out by sea to the New World. There is a chapel in the fort where the captains and officers of the slave ships and perhaps some of the overseers and go-betweens offered Christian worship. The chapel has a curious shape, the result, the guards will tell you, of having at one time been cut in two in order to provide more space for business, that is, the negotiations between those who brought the slaves down to the coast and those who transported them. There does not seem to be any evidence that the God who was worshiped in that chapel was able to work through the worshipers and help them to serve as agents of change in a cruel system. The slave trade, however, was abolished in the nineteenth century in the West, and it is generally agreed that the two chief causes of the abolition were the growing sense among Christians that it was wrong and the hard fact that with industrialization and technical progress, it had become unprofitable.

Then there is the position of women, the oppression of

minorities, and the exploitation of children. Christianity probably has had something to do with progress in these areas. History, however, shows how much cruelty a Christian society can tolerate and even generate: crusades (including some current ones), inquisitions, the torture of prisoners, and the grinding of the faces of the poor. Where is all that salt, that agent of change, that was to be at once a sign of the bond between the people of the New Covenant where natural selfishness was turned into sacrificial love, and the preserver of grace in the community, enhancing and heightening its joy and its beauty?

Society is in need of change agents. We are not very happy with the air we breathe, the noise level and violence of our environment, the proliferation of pornography, and we look with fear towards the future when we think of our dwindling natural resources and population increase—two trends that unless reversed are bound to clash and precipitate us all into an unimaginable catastrophe—if some nuclear disaster does not overtake us first.

In the most optimistic view of the world's future, a rearrangement of priorities and values could stimulate the kind of social and economic change that would save the future generations and guarantee that there would be enough for everyone. Change agents, on this view, would be needed at all levels, from the supermarket shopper to management and through all the intervening layers, up to those invisible people at the top of the economic power structure, those who make decisions and direct policy for multinational corporations. Sometimes one wonders whether there are any people there at all, or whether they have all been replaced by machinery. Let us hope that someone is there, because if the blind thrust of economic development, eating up more and more of the earth's resources, polluting more and more of the earth, the water, and the air, and turning out consumer goods for a smaller and smaller proportion of the world's population, is to be turned around and focused instead upon conservation and distribution, it will have to be done by human change agents at the very highest level.

You are the salt of the earth; but if salt has lost its taste, how shall its saltness be restored? (Mt. 5:13)

Another kind of pollution is aesthetic and moral. It is created by pornography, by ugliness, by the shoddy and tasteless products that glare at us from so many display cases and advertisements; it is created by prejudice, by the putting down of whole groups, countries, and areas because their customs and language, priorities and manners, are different from our own. Change agents are needed in this area also. Psychological experimentation has demonstrated that prejudice in a group is deepened whenever an individual expresses a prejudiced viewpoint in emotional tones. Whenever, on the other hand, in the same group the prejudice is challenged, then the negative attitudes of the group remain stable instead of increasing. In such a situation a Christian at a certain cost can serve as a change agent. The same thing holds good with regard to individuals whose good name is injured by gossip or insinuation.

Psychological pollution is demonstrated by another experiment which showed what happened to an individual headmistress when she was introduced first to a group of her colleagues who very subtly gave her a negative reception and then to another group whose manner of receiving her was much more affirmative. The first group was courteous on the surface. The leader introduced her and gave her a seat, but then the group ignored her, and whenever she tried to contribute to the conversation, she ran into an invisible barrier. Nothing she said was taken up or responded to in any depth. The whole thing made her very angry. The opposite experiment, of course, had the opposite effect. When she was really listened to, and able to make a positive contribution of her own to the group, she felt relaxed and normal. It takes only one or two members of such a group to show their superiority and their in-group status, to make the difference.

It is small things that control an atmosphere: courtesy, humor, consideration for others, putting a newcomer in touch with what has been going on, allowing a new guest or a silent member of a group to enter the conversation.

A Subtle Form of Pollution
Has to Do with Leadership and Authority

There are many ways of exercising authority, and in this fallen world all of them are dangerous. The authority of a king, for instance, needs to be exercised with great benevolence and wisdom if it is not to become oppression and cruelty—the using of others as if they were things and sacrificing them to prideful pretentions. Democratic power can easily become tyranny of a different kind, by sacrificing excellence, aspiration, and adventure to the mediocrity of a lowest common denominator. Neither model serves the common good. Jesus is a king. But what kind of king? The whole idea of kingship is turned upside down in the fourth Gospel. For us the right meaning of authority is found in self-denying love and in the abiding determination to "Bear witness to the truth," that is, to help lift the whole human enterprise into the dimension of eternity.

Leadership is a form of ministry, a way of reverencing others, accepting and affirming what they are and enabling them to become more and more fully what they are called to be. To abdicate leadership is as much a failure as to misuse it. This is true of all the ways we exercise power, from the older or stronger of two children through the multiple forms of leadership in society: policemen, teachers, office workers, up to the places of greater power, presidents and kings. For them, as for us all, the pattern endures: kingship is servanthood, and leaders are to serve the common good and not themselves.

Another symbol of the change agent which is common in Scripture is leaven. This is an equally humble and hidden symbol. It is used for both good and bad change in Scripture. It was expressly excluded from sacrifice because it was a symbol of corruption. The disciples were warned against the "leaven of the Pharisees and the Sadducees" (Mt. 16:6), that is, false teaching. Jesus uses the action of leaven in dough in the good sense as a symbol of the Kingdom. "The kingdom of heaven is like leaven which a woman took and hid in three measures of meal, till it was all leavened" (Mt. 13:33). Leaven grows secretly and transforms the dough.

Whether we like it or not, Christians are models, working patterns for those around them. They are watched under circumstances of distress, trouble, and temptation to see how they will react. Their attitudes toward individuals or groups, the kind of jokes they make, the way they deal with criticisms and setbacks, show what their priorities are and what their claims to fame. Off-the-cuff reactions and responses are more revealing than protestations of upright intentions and disclaimers of prejudice.

Leaven works secretly, not like salt, by preserving, but by breaking down. So it is with grace, the Holy Spirit of Christ, poured forth in our hearts, to break down and destroy the kingdom of sin, Satan, and death. It attacks every trace, patch, or immense field and spreading stain of corruption it finds. It does this in the secret workings going on now in each of us and in our social units, large and small. Grace also works like salt. It preserves every grain of goodness it can find and heightens its flavor.

> Have salt in yourselves, and be at peace with one another.
> The Kingdom of heaven is like leaven.

Christians as Men and Women of the Future

Christians are men and women of the future. This has been understood in many ways, including the *pie in the sky* of the old Marxist jibe as well as the more sombre evocation of the *last things:* death, judgment, heaven, and hell. Eschatology, that part of theology which deals with the ultimate in relation to creation, providence, and judgment, has been rescued from its place at the end of systematic theology and in the form of a *theology of hope* has been given a new and leading position, at least by some theologians. As we become more and more aware of the serious threats posed to the stability of the earth itself, by *development*, that is, by the growth of urban complexes, industry, and technology, theologians are turning their attention downwards and up-wards, to the land and sea and skies of our created environ-ment, hoping to find new stability in the processes of the earth themselves. They also look forward, towards a hoped-for future.

What we call eschatology developed as a theology of hope in the first place. It was after the Jews had seen the collapse of everything upon which they had pinned their hopes, the line of David, the city of Jerusalem, and the Temple, that they began to look for a different kind of king and a different kind of kingdom.

A theology of hope begins with the Holy Spirit. In the eighth chapter of Romans, Paul's great chapter on the Holy Spi·it, the focus is on the future: "For the creation waits with eager longing for the revealing of the sons of God" (Rom. 8:19). Paul describes us all as "groaning inwardly," "groan-ing in travail," waiting in patience and in hope. Over against this picture of a spirit bringing the world out of the dark void into time and space, we have another coming into view with gathering menace. Its prelude is the encroaching tide of concrete, the swelling piles of dead automobiles rusting in the sun, and the refuse of Western cities, globs of oil, broken gadgets of colored plastic, defiling the empty beaches of the African coast. Will its ultimate symbol be the black holes of anti-matter about which the space explorers tell us: vora-cious emptinesses that neutralize and destroy everything that is drawn into them?

The Christian theology of hope stands over against this symbol. It is a theology, not of reversal or even of restoration, but of resurrection by the gift of God, of the coming of a new thing, lifting created structures onto a new plane of being. It is by hope and not by sight that we are to move towards a promised future, the inheritance of the Kingdom.

One of the marks of this new stance towards the future is often designated as *openness*. We live in a time of unprecedented change, and our *lifestyles* as Christians must be open to change. We need not, however, advocate the acceptance of every new thing.

The church has always been an open community. It is called to live within the structures of the world and to respond to them. Ethics has developed as a Christian discipline in response to changing social, political, and economic structures. The beginning of industrialization and the rise of new cities, for example, produced the doctrines of *just wage and just price*. The Christian theology of our own day is engaged in the same enterprise. It struggles to understand the world in which it lives and to distinguish between what it can assimilate and what it must reject or try to change.

It is said that when the astronomer Galileo was forced to kneel and recant the proposition that the earth moves around the sun and not vice versa, he muttered under his breath as he rose from his knees, "It does too move!" The church of his day was not ready to listen to new scientific truth, and for much of her history she has come panting along, bringing up the rear, when new discoveries were made in every area of human life. Astronomy, the evolution of species, the critical study of the Bible, the development of psychiatry, sociology, and politics, all offer sad examples of experiences like that of Galileo.

One of the areas that confronts all of us is a complex sometimes called *futurology*. New prophets point out to us that world resources are limited and not limitless, and that we are rapidly approaching the limits. This is a new and unwelcome idea. It is painful and frightening; it is in fact like a great black pit opening without warning before our feet. Our reaction to black pits of whatever kind, as we have seen, tends to be denial. Our society continues to deny the reality of limits. There are different ways in which we can deny, beginning with apathy. In the face of the immensity of the problems of pollution, world hunger, overpopulation, and nuclear threat, who can fail to feel utterly helpless? The temptation is great to turn our attention elsewhere. Another form of denial is retreat to the *spiritual*, that is to say, to the spiritual understood as unworldly, subjective, and *religious*.

When we cut off part of our life, that part which is reserved for worship, meditation, and personal development, from the life of the world and of the society around us, and call it *spiritual*, we are denying the basic proclamation of Christianity, namely, that "the Word became flesh and dwelt among us."

A third form of denial exists on the intellectual and technical level, when those in policy-making positions in industry, advertising, and government do not take time to consider the evidence but go on with business as usual, pushing hard for *development*, and putting all their eggs in the basket of expanding production, regardless of environmental factors.

Some writers on ecology today, Lynn White for example, blame the Christian doctrine of creation as found in Genesis for the ecological crisis, because it encourages the domination and exploitation of the earth, of plants and the lesser animals, by the human race.

Other writers point out that the Genesis account does not imply that man is to waste and spoil, but to care for the rest of creation. Both creation myths in Genesis came from a world view far different from our own, and one in which the idea of limits had no place. It has no place anywhere in Holy Scripture; it is not until our own day that we have realized the implications for humankind of the fact that created means finite, and finite means limited. The problem that confronts us today is how to use the things of our limited world with justice.

The black hole that yawns in our path and that seems not very far away is like the other black holes in our experience, an invitation to accept the pain and humiliation of having to reduce our standard of living so that all may share in the limited resources of the world, and to find in that acceptance a transforming gift, the seed of a new society. The pattern of that society has already been given in the description in the Acts of the Apostles, the description of the church in Jerusalem, as a community that devoted itself to the teaching and fellowship of the Apostles, to the breaking of bread and of prayers, and to the community of goods.

Men and women of the future are charged with the duty of conserving and handing on to those who come after the treasures of wisdom and knowledge we have inherited, along with conservation of the earth itself. Part of this treasure has to do with the value of simplicity and sparingness, the joy to be found in the contemplation of common things, and the cultivation of inwardness and serenity. The ascetic strain in Christianity begins to seem relevant again, and even the Desert Fathers are best sellers.

The Joy of Limitation

While there are severe limits on outward growth and development, there are no limits on interior spiritual development. There are infinite possibilities for developing and enhancing the quality of life for both individuals and communities. The inward realm of human life is infinite, and it is something we have long neglected. Limitations imposed upon us by outward circumstances may well be the means by which we can all grow in other ways. Having to eat less meat, use less gasoline, be satisfied with fewer possessions, far from being terrible deprivations we are forced to endure, may well be the occasion of a new and undreamed freedom. Few of us realize how possessed we are by our possessions, how enslaved we are by our inflated standard of living. New ways of being human open up to us when we are set free from what have become for us necessities. The truth is that many of our necessities are really luxuries for most human beings. Because the future is God's future, we can embrace with hope a simpler and less cluttered way of life.

The Christian Vision of the Future

The Christian is a member of that pilgrim community which has faith in the future not out of a naive optimism but simply because the future (whatever it brings) belongs to God. The Christian vision is a lovely and impressive one: a heavenly banquet at which the whole of humanity, risen and restored in Christ, sits. It is a vision of what the Russians call *sobornost*, which means much the same as the word catholicity except that it emphasizes equality and loving collaboration. Catholicity is the word we use to describe the all-encompassing vision of Christianity and its universal claim. *Sobornost* is the quiet testimony of the common people of God who love one another in the world which God has made. More is accomplished in this quiet testimony than we will ever know. Some of us may be called to the ultimate test of martyrdom, others to a quiet and obscure witness. Each one of us is called to be a presence in the world, a sign of the future which is God's. That is why we Christians, in the face of enormous pressures, continue to live in hope.

> The world is wide and rich, complex and difficult. . . . The battle in it, the struggle upwards and inwards of life and light is slow, varied, and often checked and thrown back. Those who try to push matters on must be prepared for more or less of martyrdom. But, oh joy!—things move, things grow, light comes, and souls are helped, for all that, and all that, and not one pang, or sigh, or tear of the labourers or self-purifiers is lost or fails to go directly to help in this increase of life for souls. (Friedrich von Hügel)

Things move, things grow, light comes. This is the Christian hope in Christ. The concern of this book has been the way we human beings move and grow in and towards the light. We began with the birth of a baby. We end with an affirmation of hope in the face of death. For us our dying will be but the birth pangs drawing into a greater life, a greater light . . . through Jesus Christ, Our Lord.

Notes

CHAPTER TWO

1. Friedrich von Hügel, *Mystical Element of Religion*, 2nd ed., vol. 1 (London: J. M. Dent & Sons, 1961), p. 26.
2. Author's paraphrase.

CHAPTER FIVE

1. Gerard Manley Hopkins
2. Julian of Norwich, *Revelations of Divine Love* (Westminster, Md.: Christian classics, 1974), p. 68.

CHAPTER SEVEN

1. Anne Sexton, *The Awful Rowing toward God* (Boston: Houghton Mifflin, 1975).
2. John Scotus Erigena, P. L. CXXXII, 390.

CHAPTER TEN

1. *The Mystical Element of Religion*, 2nd ed., vol. 1 (London: J. C. Dent & Sons, 1961), p. 26.
2. New York: Harper & Row, 1974.

CHAPTER TWELVE

1. *De Civitate Dei* VIII, 17.
2. *Treatise against the Errors of Abelard* (P. L. 182:1072).
3. Robert Browning's "Bishop Bloughram's Apology"

CHAPTER THIRTEEN

1. See also Ezekiel 37:5. Here, breath equals *spirit*.

CHAPTER TWENTY

1. W. H. Auden, *Protestant Mystics,* ed. Anne Fremantle (Boston: Little Brown, 1964), p. 32.

CHAPTER TWENTY-ONE

1. p. 258 Henry Suso, *Little Book of Eternal Wisdom*.
2. Traherne
3. Donne
4. Aquinas
5. Cardinal Berulle, "Opuscules de Piété," p. 27 (p. 260).

CHAPTER TWENTY-TWO

1. Arthur Michael Ramsey, *Sacred and Secular* (New York: Harper & Row, 1965).

Suggestions
for Further Reading

There are innumerable books concerning the spiritual life in general and the life of prayer in particular. What follows is simply a list of fairly straightforward books that may be helpful to those who wish to explore this area more deeply.

The Paulist Press has published a series of books entitled *The Classics of Western Spirituality*. There are sixty volumes in the series, and not all are of equal interest. It is, nevertheless, an admirable project which will serve the church well in the years ahead.

Julian of Norwich, *Revelations of Divine Love* (Westminster, Md.: Christian Classics, 1974).

Anonymous, *The Cloud of Unknowing* (New York: Penguin, 1978).

Saint Teresa of Ávila, *The Life of Teresa of Jesus: The Autobiography of St. Teresa of Ávila* (New York: Doubleday, 1973).

Thomas Merton, *Contemplative Prayer* (New York: Doubleday, 1971), *Spiritual Direction and Meditation* (Collegeville, Minn.: Liturgical Press, 1960).

J. Neville Ward, *The Use of Praying* (New York: Oxford University Press, 1977).

James Fenhagen, *More than Wanderers* (New York: The Seabury Press, 1978).

Henri J. Nouwen, *With Open Hands* (Notre Dame, Ind.: Ave Maria Press, 1972).

Tilden Edwards, *Living Simply through the Day* (New York: Paulist Press, 1978).

Kenneth Leech, *Soul Friend: A Study of Spirituality* (New York: The British Book Center, 1977).

H. A. Williams, *The Simplicity of Prayer* (Philadelphia: Fortress Press, 1977).

William Johnston, *Silent Music* (New York: Harper & Row, 1974), *The Inner Eye of Love: Mysticism and Religion* (New York: Harper & Row, 1978).

Anthony Bloom, *Living Prayer* (Springfield, Ill.: Templegate Publishers, 1975).

Index

solitary spot, where he devoted himself to prayer, study, fasting, and the manual labor necessary to support himself. He overcame violent temptations, and in time a group of followers gathered around him. He organized them into communities and exercised a certain amount of authority over them, but he never wrote a formal rule for the monastic life. An account of his life was written by Saint Athanasius, who knew him personally.

——following of Christ, 66

Aquinas, Saint Thomas, *see* Thomas Aquinas, Saint

Ascetics, 12, 31

Auden, W. H. (1907–1973), British-American poet. He was born in York, England, the son of a physician. Both his grandfathers were Anglican clergymen. After leaving Oxford, where he was a student from 1925 to 1928, he spent a year in Germany, then returned to England and became a leader in intellectual circles. He settled in the United States in 1939, becoming an American citizen in 1946. His witty analysis of contemporary society, written from the viewpoint of a convinced Christian, made him one of the most interesting poets of his time. In addition to poems, he wrote plays, librettos, criticism, and translated Dag Hammarskjold's *Markings*. In 1948 he won the Pulitzer Prize for *The Age of Anxiety*.

——on Anglicanism, 177; on dogmatic theology, 82

Augustine, Saint (354–430), theologian and philosopher, and bishop of Hippo. He was born in Numidia, in North Africa, to a Christian woman, Monica, and a Roman official, Patricius. In Carthage, where he went to study in 370, and where he later conducted a school of rhetoric, Augustine came under the influence of the Manichean sect. In 383 he went to Rome to lecture, and the next year to Milan. He abandoned Manicheanism, and began a study of Neoplatonism. Influenced by the preaching of St. Ambrose, the bishop of Milan, and by the prayers and tears of Monica, he was baptized into the Christian Church in 387. He returned to Africa, and in 391 was ordained a priest. In 396 he was chosen bishop of Hippo. Although Augustine lived in turbulent times, he produced a vast body of work, including his *Confessions* and *The City of God*, which has been a decisive influence in the history of Western thought.

——on activity of God, 191, 219; definition of religion, 102; on the Eucharist, 122, 154; experience with mother at Ostia,

bridge, but did not take a degree. He traveled on the continent, took part in military expeditions, and from 1598 to 1602 served as secretary to the lord keeper of the great seal. Sometime during this period he became an Anglican. He was ordained in 1615, and in 1621 became dean of St. Paul's Cathedral, a post he held until his death. Donne was one of the leading Metaphysical Poets of the 17th century, and he has been a great influence on 20th century poetry. His prose works include more than 160 sermons and his *Devotions Upon Emergent Occasions*, written after a serious illness in 1623.

——poetry of, 178; on relationship with God, 191–92

Dove, symbolism of, 88

E

Eastern spirituality, 47

Ecology, *see* Environmental concerns

Economic concerns, 225, 230

Ecumenical movement, 180, 184

Election, 13–14, 130; *see also* Chosen people

English Reformation, 177

Enduring love, of God, 95

Environment, influence of, 44

Environmental concerns, 225, 230–31

Equality, 211

Erigena, John Scotus (c. 810–877), theologian and philosopher. Probably born in Ireland, around 845 he was called to France to take charge of the palace schools. He made Latin translations of Greek writings, and he produced controversial works of his own, including *On Divine Predestination* and *On the Division of Nature*. Using Neoplatonic concepts, he attempted to explain the relation of God to the created world.

——on ineffability of God, 56

Eschatology, 228–29

Ethics, 230

Eucharist, 78, 84–85, 137, 154–55; contemporary celebrations, 181–83; focus of Christian spirituality, 219; images of wisdom in, 121; in Navajo mission, 184

Evangelical party, in Anglicanism, 177

Evangelical revival, in 19th century England, 179

Evil, 50–51, 140–48

Exodus, 17–18, 29; spiritual life as, 69–70

Experience: prayer and, 67–73; transformation by, 34–35

F

Faith, 31–32; in Reformation churches, 176

False gods, 42–43

Fear of God, 131

Fellowship of the church: and baptism, 8; and prayer, 38, 119

Fénelon, François de Salignac de la Mothe (1651–1715), French archbishop and theologian.

As tutor to the grandson of Louis XIV, he advocated modern theories of education, including the education of women. His political philosophy can be found in his novel *Télémaque*, written for the private instruction of his royal pupil. He also wrote letters of spiritual counsel. After his consecration as archbishop of Cambrai in 1695, he became embroiled in the controversy over quietism, his defense of which was condemned by the pope. His treatise, *Traite de l'existence de Dieu*, written during his last years, summarizes his theological ideas.

——on ourself as gift, 58

Ferrar, Nicholas (1592–1637), English deacon. After completing his education at Cambridge and spending some years in travel and business, he retired in 1625 to Little Gidding, near Cambridge, where he founded an Anglican religious community. He was ordained a deacon in 1626. Under his direction the community followed a rule of prayer, charity, and work. It survived his death, but was broken up during the English Civil War.

——monasticism, 178

Fidelity of God, 95

Flesh, as alienation from God, 119

Following of Christ, 65–66; *see also* Imitation of Christ

Francis of Assisi, Saint (c. 1181–1226), Italian friar and founder of the Franciscan order. The son of a wealthy merchant, Francis led a frivolous, carefree life, delighting in revelry with his companions, and enjoying stories of romance and chivalry. After a severe illness, he became aware of his special calling, and he began his life of poverty, service, and preaching. In 1210 the rule which he drew up for himself and his followers was approved by Pope Innocent III. Although often sentimentalized in literature and art, St. Francis was a man of strong will and deep spiritual insight. His love of God and of all God's creation, and his joy in the practice of evangelical poverty have appealed to men and women of all backgrounds.

——on the body as "Brother Ass," 193; following of Jesus, 30

Freedom, 47, 217; and community prayer, 138; of the Holy Spirit, 127–29; and the possibility of sin, 141

Freud, Sigmund (1856–1939), Austrian neurologist and founder of psychoanalysis. His discoveries and theories, particularly in regard to the unconscious, brought new insight into the study of human behavior.

——psychotherapy, 39

ative energy, 115–16; freedom of, 127–29; as gift, 129; illumination and sanctification, 115; our relationship with, 112; and prayer, 110–16; as spiritual guide, 172; surrender to, 33, 50; temples of, 190; and theology of hope, 229; as wisdom, 121

Hooker, Richard (1554–1600), English theologian. In his major work *Treatise on the Laws of Ecclesiastical Polity*, he elaborated a theory of law based on the natural law. The treatise was published in eight volumes between 1594 and 1662. The sixth book is said to be spurious.
——middle way of, 178

Hope, 64, 215, 233; theology of, 228–29

Hopkins, Gerard Manley (1844–1889), English poet and Jesuit priest. While studying at Oxford he became interested in Catholicism, and was received into the Church in 1866. In 1868 he entered the Society of Jesus. His poems, none of which were published during his lifetime, are notable for technical innovations. Among the best known are *The Wreck of the Deutschland, God's Grandeur, Carrion Comfort,* and *Spring and Fall: To a Young Child.*
——on transformation in Christ, 44; on work of the Spirit, 125

Hügel, Baron Friedrich von (1852–1925), British Roman Catholic scholar. He was born in Florence, Italy, where his father was in the Austrian diplomatic service. The family eventually settled in England, and Baron von Hügel became a naturalized British subject. He was an important figure in the Modernist movement of the late 19th and early 20th centuries. Modernism, which was condemned by Pope Pius X in 1907, sought to reconcile church doctrine with the new developments in science and philosophy. Baron von Hügel remained deeply attached to Catholicism, and his major work, *The Mystical Element of Religion* (1908), lay outside the Modernist controversy. This monumental work is based on the life and thought of St. Catherine of Genoa, and contains a masterly exposition of the nature and unity of the spiritual life.
——definition of Christianity, 11; on hope, 233; on man's relationship with God, 77; three elements of religion, 168–69

Human, meaning and mystery of, 10, 19–20, 222; becoming human, images and metaphors of, 13–18, 28–37; elements of humanity, 53–60; existence as gift and challenge, 11, 13; human as image of God, 20–27; human as rooted in Christ, 77

Humanism, 175–76, 179

Human relationships, 152–154, 222; harmony of, 61–66

the leading textbook in psychology for many years. His philosophical investigations into man's need and search for a personal religion resulted in one of his major works, *The Varieties of Religious Experience* (1902). After the publication of *Pragmatism* (1907), he was recognized as the leading American philosopher of his time.

——notion of the once- and twice-born, 170

Jeremiah, prophet, 19, 93–94

Jerusalem: early church in, 25, 231; fall of, 18–19, 23–24

Jesus Christ: action, and prayer, 197–98; being human in Christ, 77–85; center of Christian life, 98; commitment to, and Christian spirituality, 43–44; as communication between God and man, 191; God's gift to us, 101; and the Holy Spirit, 125; human life of, 24–25; imitation of, 30–31, 101–3; meeting with, in the Eucharist, 84–85; as model of truly human, 10–11; names, titles, images of, 87–89, 96–97, 101–2; new covenant, 19; participation in, 103–4; presence in the Church, 73; in St. John's Gospel, 86–97; self-giving love, 53; Simeon's recognition of, 24; temptations of, 114; true God and true man, 89, 96-97; Word of God, 218

Jewish people: covenant, 17–18; election, 13–14; Exodus, 17–18, 29

Joel, prophet, 128

John, Saint, 169

John, Gospel of, 21–22, 86–97, 101–2, 135

John the Baptist, Saint, 92

Jubilate, 208

Julian of Norwich (c. 1342–1423), English mystic. An anchoress, probably a Benedictine, assigned to the Church of St. Julian in Norwich, she is remembered because of her book *The Revelations of Divine Love,* in which she recorded a series of visions and her reflections upon them. Her experiences are described in simple, homely terms, but they express a deep understanding of God's love for man and His abhorrence of sin.

——contemplation of hazelnut, 44–46

Jung, Carl Gustaf (1875–1961), Swiss psychologist. For a time a friend and admirer of Freud, Jung later broke with the Viennese psychoanalyst and developed his own system, which he called analytic psychology. He wrote extensively on the symbolic and mythical aspects of the personality, and on his notion of the collective unconscious.

——psychotherapy, 39

Justification, 31, 176

K

Keble, John (1792–1866), English clergyman and poet. He was ordained a priest in 1816 and